LITTLE TREATS
donuts

Elinor Klivans
Illustrations by Nanci Pappas

TABLE OF CONTENTS

A WORLD OF DONUTS

From that first piece of leftover dough that was dropped into a pot of hot fat over a crackling fire, to the hole-in-the-middle glazed donuts of today, these popular sweets have been around for centuries. The name "doughnuts" probably evolved from the Dutch, who shaped dough scraps into knots or "dough knots" before frying. Fast forward to the present day, and the word is commonly shortened to the "donuts" seen on the neon signs of street-corner sweets shops.

Donuts are made in all shapes and sizes. Cream-filled puffs of yeast dough, two-bite donut holes, classic glazed or frosted rings, and light, irregularly shaped fritters are just some of the choices that this book has to offer. It begins with recipes for the classic yeast and cake donuts that we know so well. Among them are old-fashioned maple bars; fruit-filled jelly donuts; rings of dark, sweet, devil's food cake; and donut holes dusted with cinnamon-sugar. These favorites are followed by a chapter featuring new and creative options that satisfy our modern appetite for variety. Chocolate rings flavored with spicy chile powder; crisp bacon-topped donuts; and puffs dipped in a sweet caramel glaze and topped with chopped pecans are just some of the tempting choices. The last recipe chapter illuminates a whole world of donut traditions, offering regional and international specialties. From France come sugar-dusted beignets; Italy contributes light ricotta zeppole; and Latin America lends its morning snack of long, crisp churros to dip in warm chocolate sauce; among other delights.

The most surprising fact about donuts is how easy they are to make at home. They are quick to mix, to form, and to cook, frying to crisp perfection in just a few minutes. Best of all, after cooling just briefly, it is time to eat the donuts. The recipes that follow will provide a wealth of choices to please any palate.

dough types

Although they come in many flavors and shapes, most donuts are made from one of three basic types of dough: yeast dough, cake dough, or pâte à choux. One common trait is that a plain donut, regardless of type of dough used, is not too sweet. It's the glazes, fillings, and toppings that supply most of the sweetness.

YEAST DOUGH Yeast-leavened donuts have a light, soft texture. After mixing, rolling, and cutting, they are set aside until they become soft and puffy. During this rising time the dough expands to form an airy texture that is emphasized when the donuts are fried.

CAKE DOUGH These donuts are leavened with baking powder, baking soda, or both, depending on the other dough ingredients, and both the mixing process and resulting texture is similar to that of a simple cake. Cake donuts are denser in texture than yeast-leavened donuts, but the extent of the crispiness depends on the ingredients. For example, a dough that contains cornmeal creates a crispier donut than one made with flour. Some donuts, such as drops and fritters, are made from a modified version of cake batter that is too moist and loose to roll and cut. Instead, the dough is added to the hot oil from a metal spoon to form large, irregular drops.

PÂTE À CHOUX This classic, French-style dough starts with a cooked mixture of milk or water, butter, salt, and flour. Eggs are beaten into the dough and then it is ready to be formed into the desired shapes, such as rings, ropes, or balls, and then deep-fried. The steam formed during frying creates the leavening and contributes to an especially light texture.

SPECIALTY DOUGHS Other donut batters don't fall into any of the above categories, but are the specialties of various countries around the world. For example, Italian zeppole derive their famously airy texture from a batter mixed with ricotta cheese. Indian-inspired donut balls use a large amount of dry milk powder to help absorb a spiced soaking syrup. New Orleans–style calas use a base of cooked rice to create a flavorful, textured breakfast fritter.

tools for making donuts

Making donuts at home does not necessarily mean purchasing new equipment; most of what you need you probably already have on hand in your kitchen. If you make donuts or other fried foods often, consider investing in a good-quality deep fryer, which eases the job of regulating the heat, controlling odors, and cleanup.

ELECTRIC MIXER OR FOOD PROCESSOR
A hand-held electric mixer or a stand mixer is ideal for making the donut dough. (If you do not have a stand mixer, use a food processor: Following the sequence outlined in the recipe, add the dry ingredients to the work bowl and pulse 3 or 4 times to mix. Add the liquid ingredients and process for 20 to 30 seconds to form a dough. Transfer the dough to a bowl or a work surface, according to the recipe, and proceed as directed.)

ROLLING PIN AND CUTTERS A rolling pin is the best tool for rolling dough into a flat round for cutting. Use a donut cutter or round pastry cutters in different sizes for cutting.

DEEP FRYER An electric deep fryer maintains a steady oil temperature and recovers its temperature quickly after donuts are added to the hot oil. Many deep fryers have a wire basket for lifting the finished donuts out of the oil and a lid that controls spattering and odors.

SAUTÉ PAN If you don't have a deep fryer, choose a sauté pan with straight sides that are at least 4½ inches high. The pan should also have a heavy bottom, which helps conduct heat evenly. When frying, take care that the hot oil does not spatter and burn you.

THERMOMETER A deep-frying thermometer ensures that the oil stays at the ideal frying temperature. It is equipped with a column attached to a metal casing and a clip that slips over the pan side to hold it securely. It is designed to register very high temperatures. Do not substitute an instant-read thermometer.

FRYING TOOLS A wide spatula or slotted spoon works well for sliding the donuts one at a time into the oil. The same spoon, a pair of tongs, or a wire skimmer are helpful tools for turning the donuts while frying and retrieving the finished donuts from the hot oil.

rolling and cutting donuts

Once you have mixed the ingredients to form a dough, gather the supplies you'll need for rolling and cutting, including a flat surface, plenty of flour, and a sturdy rolling pin. Be sure that your work surface is free of cracks or odors that could mar the donuts. A clean countertop or marble or plastic pastry board is ideal.

ROLL OUT THE DOUGH

Generously dust a work surface with all-purpose flour and place the dough in the center. Using a lightly floured rolling pin, roll out the dough into a circle 10 inches in diameter and ½ inch thick. Lift and turn the dough several times as you roll to prevent sticking. If the dough does stick, use a bench scraper or an icing spatula to loosen it, re-flour the work surface, and continue to roll. You can also refrigerate the dough for a few minutes to firm it, then continue to roll.

CUT OUT THE DONUTS

Using a 2½-inch, 3-inch, or other size donut cutter, cut out as many rounds as you can by firmly pressing the cutter into the dough; be sure the hole is cut out completely from the center. If the dough is sticking to the cutter, dip it lightly in flour. Gather the dough scraps, roll again, and cut out more rounds and holes. Discard the remaining scraps, as they will become tough from repeated rolling.

SET THE DONUTS ASIDE

If making yeast donuts, move them directly from the cutter to the prepared baking sheet, or use a wide spatula to transfer the donuts and holes. If making cake donuts, you can leave them on the work surface after cutting, but fry them as soon as possible to ensure the best texture.

LET THE DONUTS RISE (optional)

If making yeast donuts, cover the donuts and holes with a clean kitchen towel and let rise for 30 minutes. When ready, yeast donuts will look soft and puffy, but unlike many yeast doughs, they will not double in size.

ABOUT DONUT CUTTERS

Similar to round cookie cutters, donut cutters feature a circular tube in the center so that both the large rings and the small holes can be cut in one step. If you don't have a donut cutter, two round pastry cutters—a large one to cut a circle and a small one to cut the hole—are a good option. A water glass and a sharp paring knife will also do the trick.

deep-frying donuts

Deep-frying can seem daunting at first, but if you follow a few guidelines, it's easy to master. Use a type of oil that can be heated to a high temperature without burning, such as peanut or canola oil. And whether using a deep-fryer or sauté pan, testing the oil with a good deep-frying thermometer will ensure golden, crisp results.

HEAT UP THE OIL

Pour the oil to a depth of 2 inches into a deep-fryer or deep, heavy sauté pan. Heat the oil in the deep-fryer according to the manufacturers' instructions. Some have a built-in temperature gauge, but it's still a good idea to check its accuracy with a deep-frying thermometer. If using a sauté pan, clip the thermometer onto the pan side and warm the oil over medium-high heat until it reaches temperature called for in the recipe.

ADD THE DONUTS TO THE HOT OIL

When the oil reaches the desired temperature, use a wide spatula or slotted spoon to pick up a donut or hole from the baking sheet or work surface and slide it gently into the hot oil. Add 2–5 more donuts or holes, depending on the capacity of the fryer or pan, being careful not to splash the hot oil or crowd the frying vessel. The donuts should float to the top and puff to about double their size.

COOK THE FIRST BATCH

Deep-fry the donuts until dark golden on the first side (dark brown if making chocolate donuts), about 1½ minutes. Using tongs, a wire skimmer, or a slotted spoon, turn and fry until dark golden on the second side, about 1 minute longer. Transfer the fried donuts to paper towels to drain.

FRY THE REMAINING DONUTS

Repeat to fry the remaining donuts and holes, always allowing the oil to return to the initial frying temperature between batches. Be sure to watch the donuts carefully as they cook and never leave the kitchen. The time between just right and too much is just a matter of seconds.

WATCHING OIL TEMPERATURE

When donuts are fried at the proper temperature, they absorb little oil. If the frying temperature is too low, oil seeps into the dough, creating a soggy donut. If the oil is too hot, the outside of the donut will be overcooked. Most donuts cook best when the oil is maintained at 360°F but there are some exceptions. Chocolate donuts cook at a lower 350°F to prevent burning. Some light-textured donuts cook best at 340°F. Be sure to follow the recipe guidelines.

JELLY-FILLED DONUTS

It seems we are never too old for the small burst of jelly hidden in the middle of these comfortingly familiar treats. Making your own donuts somehow only sweetens the surprise. Don't worry if the dough seems sticky—a soft dough makes a tender donut. Just keep your work surface generously floured.

Canola or peanut oil for brushing and deep-frying

Yeast Donut Dough (page 102)

⅔ cup best-quality strawberry jelly or seedless raspberry, apricot, or blueberry jam

½ cup superfine sugar

MAKES ABOUT
15 DONUTS

1 Line a baking sheet with waxed paper and brush the paper with oil. Line a second baking sheet with paper towels.

2 Turn the dough out onto a generously floured work surface. Using a floured rolling pin, roll out the dough into a circle about 10 inches in diameter and ½ inch thick. Using a 3-inch round pastry cutter, cut out as many rounds as possible. Use a wide spatula to transfer the donuts to the oiled paper. Gather up the scraps and repeat rolling and cutting out donuts. Cover the donuts with a clean kitchen towel and let rise for 30 minutes. The donuts should look soft and puffy, but will not double in size.

3 Pour oil to a depth of 2 inches into a deep-fryer or deep, heavy sauté pan and heat until the oil reads 360°F on a deep-frying thermometer. Carefully lower 2–5 donuts into the hot oil and deep-fry until dark golden in color, about 1½ minutes. Turn over and cook until dark golden on the second side, about 1 minute longer. Transfer to the towel-lined baking sheet. Repeat to fry the remaining donuts, allowing the oil to return to 360°F between batches. (For more information on deep-frying, see page 13.)

4 Spread the sugar on a large plate or in a wide, shallow bowl. When the donuts are cool enough to handle, roll them in the sugar to coat on all sides. Fit a pastry bag with a ¼-inch round tip and spoon the jelly into the bag. Using the tip of a small, sharp knife, cut a ½-inch slit in the side of each donut. Press the tip of the pastry bag gently into the slits and pipe about 2 teaspoons of the jelly into each donut. Arrange the donuts on a platter and serve right away.

VANILLA-GLAZED DONUTS

For many people, this iconic ringed cake, raised feather-light with yeast and covered with a sweet vanilla glaze, is the very definition of a donut. For a change of pace, garnish the glazed donuts with a scattering of crumbled freeze-dried raspberries.

Canola or peanut oil for brushing and deep-frying

Yeast Donut Dough (page 102)

Vanilla Glaze (page 107)

½ cup freeze-dried raspberries, optional

MAKES ABOUT
15 DONUTS AND
THEIR HOLES

1 Line a baking sheet with waxed paper and brush the paper with oil. Line a second baking sheet with paper towels.

2 On a generously floured work surface, roll out the dough into a circle 10 inches in diameter and ½ inch thick. Using a 3-inch round donut cutter, cut out as many donuts as possible. Transfer the donuts and holes to the oiled paper. Gather up the donut scraps and repeat rolling and cutting. (For more information on rolling and cutting, see page 10.) Cover the donuts and holes with a clean kitchen towel and let rise until soft and puffy, about 30 minutes.

3 Pour oil to a depth of 2 inches into a deep-fryer or deep, heavy sauté pan and warm over medium-high heat until it reads 360°F on a deep-frying thermometer. Carefully lower 2–5 donuts or holes into the hot oil and deep-fry until dark golden, about 1½ minutes. Turn over and cook until dark golden on the second side, about 1 minute longer. Transfer to the towel-lined baking sheet. Repeat to fry the remaining donuts and holes, allowing the oil to return to 360°F between batches. (For more information on deep-frying, see page 13.)

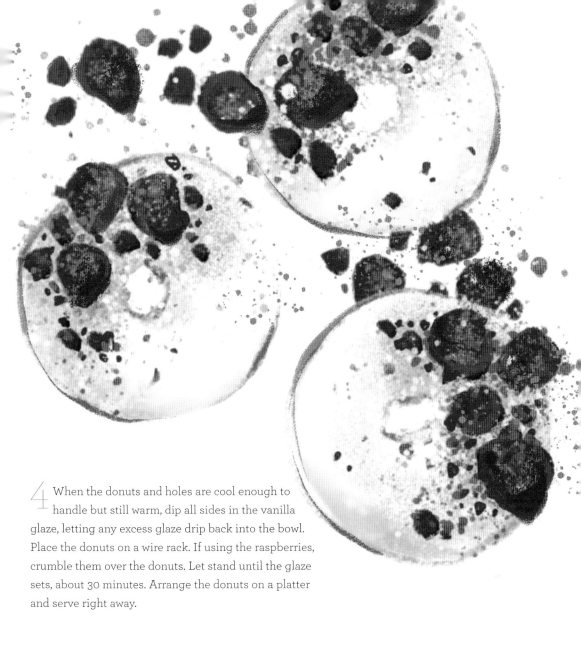

4 When the donuts and holes are cool enough to handle but still warm, dip all sides in the vanilla glaze, letting any excess glaze drip back into the bowl. Place the donuts on a wire rack. If using the raspberries, crumble them over the donuts. Let stand until the glaze sets, about 30 minutes. Arrange the donuts on a platter and serve right away.

OLD-FASHIONED
BUTTERMILK DONUTS

These classic cake donuts with a tang of buttermilk recall the golden piles in favorite bakeries of childhood memories. Leavened with baking soda and baking powder, they take minutes to mix. A combination of all-purpose flour and cake flour adds to the tender texture.

1 In a large bowl, sift together the flours, baking powder, baking soda, nutmeg, and salt. In another large bowl, using an electric mixer set on low speed (use the paddle attachment for a stand mixer), beat the egg and granulated sugar until creamy and pale in color. Add the buttermilk, melted butter, and vanilla and beat until well blended. Add the flour mixture and beat, still on low speed, just until the mixture comes together into a soft dough. Cover and refrigerate the dough until firm, at least 30 minutes and up to 1 hour.

2 Line a baking sheet with paper towels. Pour oil to a depth of 2 inches into a deep-fryer or deep, heavy sauté pan and warm over medium-high heat until it reads 360°F on a deep-frying thermometer.

continued on next page →

1¼ cups all-purpose flour

1 cup cake flour

1 teaspoon baking powder

½ teaspoon baking soda

½ teaspoon freshly grated nutmeg

½ teaspoon salt

1 large egg

½ cup granulated sugar

½ cup buttermilk

1 tablespoon unsalted butter, melted

1 teaspoon vanilla extract

Canola or peanut oil for deep-frying

Confectioners' sugar for dusting

MAKES ABOUT
10 DONUTS AND
THEIR HOLES

3 On a generously floured work surface, roll out the dough into a circle 10 inches in diameter and ½ inch thick. Using a 3-inch round donut cutter, cut out as many donuts as possible. Gather up the donut scraps and repeat rolling and cutting. (For more information on rolling and cutting, see page 10.)

4 Carefully lower 2–5 donuts or holes into the hot oil and deep-fry until dark golden, about 1½ minutes. Turn over and cook until dark golden on the second side, about 1 minute longer. Transfer to the towel-lined baking sheet to cool. Repeat to fry the remaining donuts and holes, allowing the oil to return to 360°F between batches. (For more information on deep-frying, see page 13.)

5 Arrange the donuts and holes on a platter. Using a fine-mesh sieve, dust generously with confectioners' sugar. Serve right away.

CIDER-GLAZED DONUTS

The flavors in these spiced donuts are echoed in the sweet apple cider glaze, making them especially welcome during the apple harvest in autumn. Use the season's freshly pressed cider in the glaze and accompany the donuts with more cider—even hard cider—to drink.

1 In a large bowl, sift together the flour, baking powder, cinnamon, nutmeg, allspice, and salt. In a large bowl, using an electric mixer set on low speed (use the paddle attachment for a stand mixer), beat the eggs and sugar until creamy and pale. Add half of the flour mixture and beat just until incorporated. Add the milk, melted butter, and vanilla and beat until well blended. Add the remaining flour mixture and beat, still on low speed, just until the mixture comes together into a soft dough. Cover and refrigerate the dough until firm to the touch, at least 30 minutes and up to 1 hour.

2 Line a large baking sheet with paper towels. Pour oil to a depth of 2 inches into a deep-fryer or deep, heavy sauté pan. Warm over medium-high heat until it reads 360°F on a deep-frying thermometer.

3 On a generously floured work surface, roll out the dough into a circle about 10 inches in diameter and ½ inch thick. Using a 3-inch round donut cutter, cut out as many donuts as possible. Gather up the donut scraps and repeat rolling and cutting. (For more information on rolling and cutting, see page 10.)

1¼ cups all-purpose flour

1½ teaspoons baking powder

¾ teaspoon ground cinnamon

½ teaspoon freshly grated nutmeg

½ teaspoon ground allspice

½ teaspoon salt

2 large eggs

½ cup granulated sugar

½ cup whole milk

2 tablespoons unsalted butter, melted

1 teaspoon vanilla extract

Canola or peanut oil for deep-frying

continued on next page →

4 Carefully lower 2–5 donuts or holes into the hot oil and deep-fry until dark golden, about 1½ minutes. Turn over and cook until dark golden on the second side, about 1 minute longer. Transfer to the towel-lined baking sheet. Repeat to fry the remaining donuts and holes, allowing the oil to return to 360°F between batches. (For more information on deep-frying, see page 13.)

5 To make the cider glaze, in a bowl, stir together the confectioners' sugar, cinnamon, corn syrup, vanilla, and cider until well blended. Stir in 1–2 teaspoons more cider if needed to make a smooth glaze that is easy to spread, but thick enough to cling to the donuts.

6 Using a thin metal spatula, spread about 2 tablespoons of the glaze over the top of each donut. Spread the tops of the donut holes with 1–2 teaspoons of the glaze, or dip their tops in it. Place the donuts on a wire rack, sprinkle with candy confetti, if using, and let stand until the glaze sets, about 10 minutes.

7 Arrange the donuts and holes on a platter and serve right away.

CIDER GLAZE

2 cups (8 oz/250 g) confectioners' sugar

¼ teaspoon ground cinnamon

1 teaspoon light corn syrup

¼ teaspoon vanilla extract

3 tablespoons apple cider, plus more as needed

Candy confetti for garnish (optional)

MAKES ABOUT 10 DONUTS AND THEIR HOLES

SOUR-CREAM BLUEBERRY DROPS

These blueberry-studded, two-bite donut drops are made from a thick batter that, when fried, forms an ultra-crisp crust. A coating of cinnamon-sugar gives them a sweet-spicy finish. Be sure the batter completely covers the blueberries; any exposed berries could dislodge and float in the hot oil.

2 cups all-purpose flour

1¼ teaspoons ground cinnamon

½ teaspoon baking powder

½ teaspoon baking soda

½ teaspoon salt

¾ cup sour cream

1 large egg

⅔ cup granulated sugar

1 teaspoon vanilla extract

Canola or peanut oil for deep-frying

½ cup fresh or thawed frozen unsweetened blueberries

¼ cup confectioners' sugar

MAKES ABOUT 16 DROPS

1 In a large bowl, sift together the flour, 1 teaspoon of the cinnamon, the baking powder, baking soda, and salt. In another large bowl, whisk together the sour cream, egg, granulated sugar, and vanilla until creamy and pale. Add the flour mixture and, using a large spoon, stir just until incorporated. The batter will be smooth.

2 Line a baking sheet with paper towels. Pour oil to a depth of 2 inches into a deep-fryer or deep, heavy sauté pan and warm over medium-high heat until it reads 340°F on a deep-frying thermometer.

3 Using a metal spoon, scoop up a rounded tablespoonful of the batter and poke 3 blueberries into it, spacing them evenly. The blueberries should be completely covered by the batter. Drop gently into the hot oil, or scrape in using a second spoon. Repeat to add 4 or 5 more spoonfuls to the oil. Be sure not to overcrowd the pan. The drops should float to the top and puff to just about double their size. Deep-fry until dark golden on the first side, about 2 minutes. Using

tongs, a wire skimmer, or a slotted spoon, turn and fry until dark golden on the second side, about 1½ minutes longer. Transfer to the towel-lined baking sheet to drain. Repeat to fry the remaining drops, allowing the oil to return to 340°F between batches. (For more information on deep-frying, see page 13.)

4 In a small bowl, combine the confectioners' sugar and the remaining ¼ teaspoon cinnamon and stir to mix well. Arrange the drops on a platter. Using a fine-mesh sieve, dust evenly with the cinnamon-sugar mixture. Serve right away.

TOASTED COCONUT DONUTS

These cake donuts represent a category called "sweet-milk donuts," which replaces the typical buttermilk with regular milk. The resulting mellow flavor complements the tropical sugars of the coconut glaze and the toasted coconut coating, which in turn contrasts nicely with the soft crumb of the donuts.

1 In a bowl, sift together the flour, baking powder, and salt. In a large bowl, using an electric mixer set on low speed (use the paddle attachment for a stand mixer), beat the eggs and sugar until creamy. Add half of the flour mixture and beat until incorporated. Add the milk, melted butter, and vanilla and beat until well blended. Add the remaining flour mixture and beat, still on low speed, just until the mixture comes together into a soft dough. Cover and refrigerate the dough until firm, at least 30 minutes and up to 1 hour.

2 Line a baking sheet with paper towels. Pour oil to a depth of 2 inches into a deep-fryer or deep, heavy sauté pan and warm over medium-high heat until it reads 360°F on a deep-frying thermometer.

3 On a generously floured work surface, roll out the dough into a circle 10 inches in diameter and ½ inch thick. Using a 2½-inch or 3-inch round donut cutter, cut out as many donuts as possible. Gather up the donut scraps and repeat rolling and cutting. (For more information on rolling and cutting, see page 10.)

4 Carefully lower 2–5 donuts or holes into the hot oil and deep-fry until dark golden, about 1½ minutes. Turn over and cook until

2¼ cups all-purpose flour

1½ teaspoons baking powder

½ teaspoon salt

2 large eggs

½ cup granulated sugar

½ cup whole milk

2 tablespoons unsalted butter, melted

1 teaspoon vanilla extract

Canola or peanut oil for deep-frying

Coconut Glaze (page 107)

3 cups sweetened shredded coconut, toasted (page 102)

MAKES ABOUT 10 DONUTS AND THEIR HOLES

continued on next page →

dark golden on the second side, about 1 minute longer. Transfer to the towel-lined baking sheet. Repeat to fry the remaining donuts and holes, allowing the oil to return to 360°F between batches. (For more information on deep-frying, see page 13.)

5 When the donuts and holes are cool enough to handle but still warm, dip all sides in the coconut glaze, letting any excess glaze drip back into the bowl. Place on a wire rack and let stand for about 10 minutes. Roll the donuts and holes in the toasted coconut to lightly coat all sides. Serve right away.

CINNAMON TWISTS

Folding ropes of this pliable yeast dough and giving them a couple of twists is a simple task that yields a spectacular effect. The silky cinnamon glaze coats all of the swirled nooks and crannies of these perennial favorites. Serve them with freshly brewed coffee and you have the perfect morning treat.

1 In a saucepan over medium heat, combine the milk and butter and heat, stirring, until the butter melts and the mixture is hot but not boiling (about 125°F on an instant-read thermometer). Remove from the heat and set aside.

2 Fit a stand mixer with the paddle attachment. In the mixing bowl, combine 2½ cups of the flour, the granulated sugar, cinnamon, salt, and yeast and beat on low speed to mix. Add the hot milk mixture, raise the speed to medium, and beat until well blended and smooth. Add the eggs and vanilla and beat until incorporated, about 2 minutes. Add the remaining ¾ cup flour and beat until well blended and smooth, about 1 minute longer. The dough will not pull away from the sides of the bowl and will still be somewhat sticky, but your finger should come out clean when you insert it into the center. (For a food processor method, see page 9.)

3 Scrape the dough into a large bowl and cover with a clean kitchen towel. Let stand in a warm place until well risen and increased in bulk (it may almost double in size), about 45 minutes.

¾ cup whole milk

3 tablespoons unsalted butter

3¼ cups all-purpose flour

⅓ cup granulated sugar

1½ teaspoons ground cinnamon

½ teaspoon salt

1 package (2½ teaspoons) quick-rise yeast

2 large eggs

½ teaspoon vanilla extract

Canola or peanut oil for brushing and deep-frying

Cinnamon Glaze (page 107)

Cinnamon-sugar for dusting (optional)

MAKES 18 TWISTS

continued on next page →

4 Line a baking sheet with waxed paper and brush the paper with oil. Line a second baking sheet with paper towels.

5 Turn the dough out onto a generously floured work surface. Using a floured rolling pin, roll out the dough into an 18-by-9-inch rectangle. Using a large, sharp knife, cut the rectangle into 18 strips, each about 9 inches long and 1 inch wide. Bend each strip in half and twist the dough halves around each other 3 or 4 times to make a tight spiral. Pinch the ends to seal and place on the oiled paper. Cover with a clean kitchen towel and let rise for 30 minutes. The twists should look soft and puffy, but will not double in size.

6 Pour oil to a depth of 2 inches into a deep-fryer or deep, heavy sauté pan and warm over medium-high heat until it reads 360°F on a deep-frying thermometer. Carefully lower 2–5 twists into the oil and deep-fry until dark golden, about 1½ minutes. Turn over and cook until dark golden on the second side, about 1 minute longer. Transfer to the towel-lined baking sheet. Repeat to fry the remaining donuts, allowing the oil to return to 360°F between batches. (For more information on deep-frying, see page 13.)

7 When the donuts are cool enough to handle but still warm, dip all sides in the cinnamon glaze, letting any excess glaze drip back into the bowl. (You may not use all of the glaze, but this makes for easier dipping.) Place on a wire rack, sprinkle with the cinnamon-sugar, if using, and let stand until the glaze sets, about 30 minutes. Arrange on a platter and serve right away.

APPLE FRITTERS

Apple fritters vary in form, from apple slices dipped in batter and fried to batters enriched with chopped apples like these. The outside of these generous fritters is roughly textured—just right for capturing the cinnamon-apple glaze.

1 cup all-purpose flour

¼ cup granulated sugar

1 teaspoon baking powder

¾ teaspoon ground cinnamon

½ teaspoon salt

⅓ cup whole milk

1 large egg, lightly beaten

1 tablespoon lemon juice

½ teaspoon grated lemon zest

½ teaspoon vanilla extract

1 large apple, cored, peeled, and finely chopped

Canola or peanut oil for deep-frying

Cinnamon-Apple Glaze (page 107)

MAKES ABOUT 24 FRITTERS

1 In a large bowl, whisk together the flour, sugar, baking powder, cinnamon, and salt. Make a well in the center of the flour mixture. Add the milk, egg, lemon juice and zest, and vanilla to the well and stir with a fork until well blended. Add the apple and stir just until evenly distributed.

2 Line a large baking sheet with paper towels. Pour oil to a depth of 2 inches into a deep-fryer or deep, heavy sauté pan and warm over medium-high heat until it reads 360°F on a deep-frying thermometer.

3 Using a metal spoon, scoop up a rounded tablespoonful of the batter and drop into the hot oil, or scrape in using a second spoon. Repeat to add 5 or 6 more fritters to the oil. Be sure not to overcrowd the pan. The fritters should float to the top and puff to about double their size. Deep-fry until dark golden on the first side, about 2 minutes. Using tongs, a wire skimmer, or a slotted spoon, turn and fry until dark golden on the second side, about 1 minute longer. Transfer to the towel-lined baking sheet to drain. Repeat to fry the remaining fritters, allowing the oil to return to 360°F between batches. (For more information on deep-frying, see page 13.)

GLAZED ORANGE BLOSSOMS

These unique, beautifully shaped, half-size donuts are created by cutting slits into the tops of balls of yeast dough; while rising, the sections open like the blossoms of a flower. Orange flower water delicately scents the dipping glaze.

¾ cup whole milk

3 tablespoons unsalted butter

3¼ cups all-purpose flour

⅓ cup granulated sugar

½ teaspoon salt

1 package (2½ teaspoons) quick-rise yeast

2 large eggs

2 teaspoons grated orange zest

½ teaspoon vanilla extract

Canola or peanut oil for brushing and deep-frying

Orange-Flower Glaze (page 106)

½ cup edible blossoms, optional

MAKES ABOUT
18–20 DONUTS

1 In a small saucepan over medium heat, combine the milk and butter. Heat, stirring, until the butter melts and the mixture is hot but not boiling (about 125°F on an instant-read thermometer). Remove the pan from the heat and set aside.

2 Fit a stand mixer with the paddle attachment. In the mixing bowl, combine 2½ cups of the flour, the sugar, salt, and yeast and beat on low speed to mix. Add the hot milk mixture, raise the speed to medium, and beat until well blended. Add the eggs, orange zest, and vanilla and beat until fully incorporated, about 2 minutes. Add the remaining ¾ cup flour and beat until well blended and smooth, about 1 minute longer. The dough will not pull away from the sides of the bowl and will still be somewhat sticky, but your finger should come out clean when you insert it into the center.

3 Scrape the dough into a large bowl and cover with a clean kitchen towel. Let stand in a warm place until well risen and increased in bulk (it may almost double in size), about 45 minutes.

4 Line a baking sheet with waxed paper and brush the paper with oil. Line a second baking sheet with paper towels.

continued on next page →

5 Lightly grease the palms of your hands with oil. Pull off about 2 teaspoons of the dough and roll it between your palms into a smooth ball about 1½ inches in diameter. Place it on the greased paper. Repeat to shape the remaining dough, spacing the balls 1–2 inches apart on the baking sheet. You should have about 18–20 donut balls. Using a sharp knife, cut 2 evenly spaced horizontal slits and then 2 evenly spaced vertical slits into the top of each ball, making sure to penetrate halfway through the dough ball. Cover again with a clean kitchen towel and let rise for 30 minutes. The donuts should look soft and puffy, but will not double in size. The slits should spread open as the dough rises.

6 Pour oil to a depth of 2 inches into a deep-fryer or deep, heavy sauté pan and warm over medium-high heat until it reads 360°F on a deep-frying thermometer. Carefully transfer 2–5 of the blossoms into the hot oil and deep-fry until dark golden, about 2 minutes. Using tongs, a wire skimmer, or a slotted spoon, turn over and cook for 1½ minutes longer. Transfer to the towel-lined baking sheet. Repeat to fry the remaining donuts, allowing the oil to return to 360°F between batches. (For more information on deep-frying, see page 13.)

7 When the donuts are cool enough to handle but still warm, dip the tops in the orange-flower glaze, letting any excess glaze drip back into the bowl. (You may not use all of the glaze, but this makes for easier dipping.) Place on a wire rack, glaze side up, and sprinkle with the blossoms, if using. Let stand until the glaze sets, about 30 minutes. Arrange on a platter and serve right away.

MAPLE BARS

Maple syrup adds an inviting golden color and a taste evoking Sunday breakfast to the thick glaze that gilds these donuts. Use a long, sharp knife in a firm downward motion to cut the sticky dough into neat bar shapes.

Canola or peanut oil for brushing and deep-frying

Yeast Donut Dough (page 102)

Maple Glaze (page 108)

Chocolate Glaze (page 108), optional

MAKES 12 BARS

1 Line a baking sheet with waxed paper and brush the paper with oil. Line a second baking sheet with paper towels.

2 Turn the dough out onto a generously floured work surface. Using a floured rolling pin, roll out the dough into a 12-by-8-inch rectangle. Using a sharp knife, cut the rectangle into 12 bars, each about 4 inches long and 2 inches wide. Use a wide spatula to transfer the bars to the oiled paper. Cover the bars with a clean kitchen towel and let rise for 30 minutes. The bars should look soft and puffy, but will not double in size.

3 Pour oil to a depth of 2 inches into a deep-fryer or deep, heavy sauté pan and warm over medium-high heat until it reads 360°F on a deep-frying thermometer. Carefully lower 2–5 bars into the oil and deep-fry until dark golden in color, about 1½ minutes. Turn over and cook until dark golden in color on the second side, about 1 minute longer. Transfer to the towel-lined baking sheet. Repeat to fry the remaining bars, allowing the oil to return to 360°F between batches.

4 When the bars are cool enough to handle, place them on a wire rack. Dip one side of the donuts into the maple glaze, then drizzle with the chocolate glaze, if using. Let stand until the glaze is set, about 10 minutes, then serve.

CINNAMON-SUGAR DONUT HOLES

Here, donut holes are promoted from assistant to head honcho. To form the "holes," spoonfuls of dough are rolled between the palms of your hands into a crowd's worth of delicious round mini donuts. If not eaten right away, these are still tasty the next day; just warm them for 5–7 minutes in a 300°F oven.

2¼ cups all-purpose flour

2 teaspoons ground cinnamon

1½ teaspoons baking powder

½ teaspoon salt

2 large eggs

1½ cups granulated sugar

½ cup whole milk

2 tablespoons unsalted butter, melted

1 teaspoon vanilla extract

Canola or peanut oil for brushing and deep-frying

MAKES ABOUT 40 HOLES

1 In a bowl, sift together the flour, 1 teaspoon of the cinnamon, the baking powder, and the salt.

2 In a large bowl, using an electric mixer set on low speed (use the paddle attachment for a stand mixer), beat the eggs and ½ cup of the sugar until creamy and pale. Add half of the flour mixture and beat just until incorporated. Add the milk, melted butter, and vanilla and beat until well blended. Add the remaining flour mixture and beat, still on low speed, just until the mixture comes together into a soft dough. Cover and refrigerate the dough until firm to the touch, at least 30 minutes and up to 1 hour.

3 Line a baking sheet with waxed paper and brush the paper with oil. Line a second baking sheet with paper towels. Pour oil to a depth of 2 inches into a deep-fryer or deep, heavy sauté pan and warm over medium-high heat until it reads 360°F on a deep-frying thermometer.

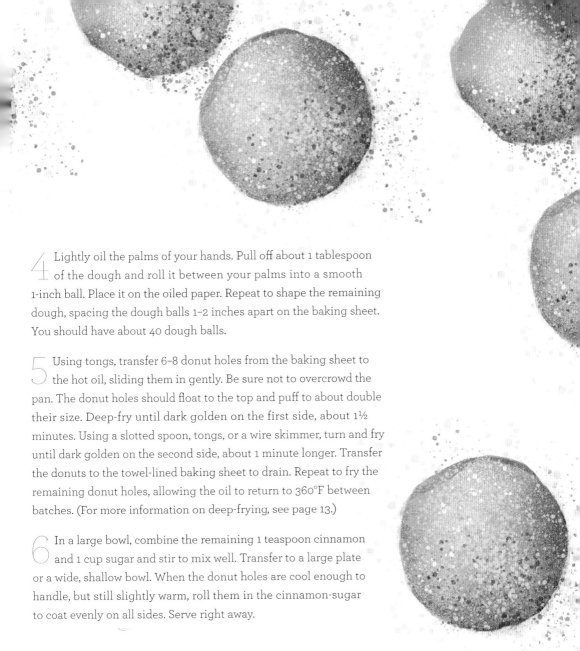

4   Lightly oil the palms of your hands. Pull off about 1 tablespoon of the dough and roll it between your palms into a smooth 1-inch ball. Place it on the oiled paper. Repeat to shape the remaining dough, spacing the dough balls 1–2 inches apart on the baking sheet. You should have about 40 dough balls.

5   Using tongs, transfer 6–8 donut holes from the baking sheet to the hot oil, sliding them in gently. Be sure not to overcrowd the pan. The donut holes should float to the top and puff to about double their size. Deep-fry until dark golden on the first side, about 1½ minutes. Using a slotted spoon, tongs, or a wire skimmer, turn and fry until dark golden on the second side, about 1 minute longer. Transfer the donuts to the towel-lined baking sheet to drain. Repeat to fry the remaining donut holes, allowing the oil to return to 360°F between batches. (For more information on deep-frying, see page 13.)

6   In a large bowl, combine the remaining 1 teaspoon cinnamon and 1 cup sugar and stir to mix well. Transfer to a large plate or a wide, shallow bowl. When the donut holes are cool enough to handle, but still slightly warm, roll them in the cinnamon-sugar to coat evenly on all sides. Serve right away.

POTATO DONUTS

Old-fashioned and modern come together in these classic donuts: Mashed potatoes lend an uncommonly smooth texture, and mace—a spice made from the outer covering of nutmeg berries with, logically, a mild nutmeg flavor— adds aroma and herbal hints. Salt and pepper add an unexpected savory kick.

1 In a bowl, sift together the flour, baking powder, ¾ teaspoon of the salt, ¼ teaspoon of the pepper, and the mace. In another bowl, combine the potato, ⅓ cup of the sugar, the eggs, milk, melted butter, and lemon zest. Using an electric mixer set on low speed (use the paddle attachment for a stand mixer), beat until blended. Add the flour mixture and beat until the mixture comes together into a sticky dough. Cover and refrigerate the dough until firm, at least 1 hour and up to 2 hours.

2 Line a baking sheet with paper towels. Pour oil to a depth of 2 inches into a deep fryer or deep, heavy sauté pan and warm over medium-high heat until it reads 360°F on a deep-frying thermometer.

3 On a generously floured work surface, roll out the dough into a circle 10 inches in diameter and ½ inch thick. Using a 2½-inch or 3-inch round donut cutter, cut out as many donuts as possible. Gather up the donut scraps and repeat rolling and cutting. (For more information on rolling and cutting, see page 13.)

continued on next page →

2 cups all-purpose flour

1½ teaspoons baking powder

1 teaspoon salt

¾ teaspoon freshly ground pepper

½ teaspoon ground mace

1 cup cooked, mashed, and cooled russet potato (about 1 medium potato)

⅔ cup granulated sugar

2 large eggs, lightly beaten

¼ cup whole milk

2 tablespoons unsalted butter, melted

1 teaspoon grated lemon zest

Canola or peanut oil for deep-frying

**Edible blossoms,
for garnish (optional)**

MAKES 10–12 DONUTS
AND THEIR HOLES

4 Carefully lower 2–5 donuts or holes into the hot oil and deep-fry until dark golden, about 1½ minutes. Turn over and cook until dark golden on the second side, about 1 minute longer. Transfer to the towel-lined baking sheet. Repeat to fry the remaining donuts and holes, allowing the oil to return to 360°F between batches. (For more information on deep-frying, see page 13.)

5 In a wide, shallow bowl, combine the remaining ⅓ cup sugar, ¼ teaspoon salt, and ½ teaspoon pepper and stir to mix well. When the donuts and holes are cool enough to handle, roll them in the sugar mixture to coat on all sides. Arrange on a platter, sprinkle with blossoms, if using, and serve right away.

DEVIL'S FOOD DONUTS

"Totally chocolate" perfectly describes these chocolate buttermilk donuts dipped in a luscious chocolate glaze. The glaze is the perfect consistency for decorating: try adding some chocolate sprinkles, shaved bittersweet chocolate, melted white chocolate, or chocolate curls on the glaze before it sets.

1 In a bowl, sift together the flours, cocoa powder, baking powder, baking soda, and salt. In a large bowl, using an electric mixer set on low speed (use the paddle attachment for a stand mixer), beat the egg and sugar until creamy and pale. Add the buttermilk, melted butter, and vanilla and beat until well blended and smooth. Add the flour mixture and beat, still on low speed, just until the mixture comes together into a soft dough. Cover and refrigerate the dough until firm, at least 30 minutes and up to 1 hour.

2 Line a large baking sheet with paper towels. Pour oil to a depth of 2 inches into a deep-fryer or deep, heavy sauté pan and warm over medium-high heat until it reads 360°F on a deep-frying thermometer.

3 On a floured work surface, roll out the dough into a circle 10 inches in diameter and ½ inch thick. Using a 2½-inch round donut cutter, cut out as many donuts as possible. Gather up the donut scraps and repeat rolling and cutting. (For more information on rolling and cutting, see page 10.)

continued on next page →

1 cup all-purpose flour

1 cup cake flour

¼ cup unsweetened cocoa powder, preferably Dutch process

1 teaspoon baking powder

½ teaspoon baking soda

½ teaspoon salt

1 large egg

½ cup granulated sugar

½ cup buttermilk

1 tablespoon unsalted butter, melted

1 teaspoon vanilla extract

Canola or peanut oil for deep-frying

Chocolate Glaze (page 108)

MAKES ABOUT 12 DONUTS AND THEIR HOLES

4 Carefully lower 2–5 donuts or holes into the hot oil and deep-fry until dark brown and crusty on the first side, about 1½ minutes. Turn over and cook until dark brown and crusty on the second side, about 1 minute longer. Transfer to the towel-lined baking sheet. Repeat to fry the remaining donuts and holes, allowing the oil to return to 360°F between batches. (For more information on deep-frying, see page 13.)

5 When the donuts and holes are cool enough to handle, dip the tops in the chocolate glaze, letting any excess glaze drip back into the bowl. Let stand until the glaze sets slightly, about 10 minutes. Serve right away.

PISTACHIO-ORANGE DONUTS

Chopped pistachios provide both a crunchy topping and a great complement to these orange-flavored donuts. Shelled roasted, salted pistachio nuts can be found in many kitchen specialty shops and in supermarkets. If you can only find unsalted nuts, sprinkle a few grains of salt lightly over the tops.

1 In a bowl, sift together the flour, baking powder, and salt. In a large bowl, using an electric mixer set on low speed (use the paddle attachment for a stand mixer), beat the eggs and sugar until creamy and pale. Add half of the flour mixture and beat just until incorporated. Add the milk, orange juice and zest, melted butter, and vanilla and beat until well blended. Add the remaining flour mixture and beat, still on low speed, just until the mixture comes together into a soft dough. Cover and refrigerate the dough until firm, at least 30 minutes and up to 1 hour.

2 Line a large baking sheet with paper towels. Pour oil to a depth of 2 inches into a deep-fryer or deep, heavy sauté pan. Warm over medium-high heat until it reads 360°F on a deep-frying thermometer.

3 On a floured work surface, roll out the dough into a circle 10 inches in diameter and ½ inch thick. Using an assortment of small, medium, and large round donut cutters, cut out as many donuts as possible. Gather up the donut scraps and repeat rolling and cutting. (For more information on rolling and cutting, see page 10.)

2¼ cups all-purpose flour

1½ teaspoons baking powder

½ teaspoon salt

2 large eggs

½ cup granulated sugar

¼ cup whole milk

¼ cup fresh orange juice

2 teaspoons grated orange zest

2 tablespoons unsalted butter, melted

1 teaspoon vanilla extract

Canola or peanut oil for deep-frying

continued on next page →

ORANGE GLAZE

6 tablespoons unsalted butter, melted

2½ cups confectioners' sugar

1 teaspoon vanilla extract

½ teaspoon almond extract

2 tablespoons fresh orange juice

3 tablespoons hot water, plus more as needed

1 teaspoon grated orange zest

2½ cups roasted, salted pistachio nuts, finely chopped

MAKES ABOUT 10–12 DONUTS AND THEIR HOLES

4 Carefully lower 2–5 donuts or holes into the hot oil and deep-fry until dark golden, about 1½ minutes. Turn over and cook until dark golden on the second side, about 1 minute longer. Transfer to the towel-lined baking sheet. Repeat to fry the remaining donuts and holes, allowing the oil to return to 360°F between batches. (For more information on deep-frying, see page 13.)

5 To make the orange glaze, in a bowl, whisk together the melted butter, confectioners' sugar, vanilla extract, almond extract, orange juice, and 3 tablespoons hot water until smooth. Whisk in 1–2 teaspoons more hot water if needed to give the glaze a thin consistency. Stir in the orange zest.

6 When the donuts and holes are cool enough to handle but still warm, dip the tops in the orange glaze, letting any excess glaze drip back into the bowl. (You may not use all of the glaze, but this makes for easier dipping.) Place on a wire rack and let stand until the glaze sets slightly, about 10 minutes. Put the pistachios on a large plate or in a wide, shallow bowl. Dip the tops of the donuts and donut holes in the nuts to coat the tops. Press gently with your fingertips to help them adhere, if necessary. Tap the donuts gently to shake off any loose nut pieces. Arrange on a platter and serve right away.

LEMON–OLIVE OIL DONUTS

The addition of olive oil to the dough produces a donut with earthy flavor and unique texture. The inside is especially tender and the outside crisp and crusty.

1 In a large bowl, sift together the flour, sugar, baking powder, and salt. Stir in the pepper. Make a well in the center of the flour mixture. Add the eggs, milk, olive oil, and lemon zest to the well and stir with a fork until well blended. Cover the bowl with plastic wrap and refrigerate the dough until firm, at least 30 minutes and up to 1 hour.

2 Line a large baking sheet with paper towels. Pour oil to a depth of 2 inches into a deep-fryer or deep, heavy sauté pan and warm over medium-high heat until it reads 360°F on a deep-frying thermometer.

3 On a generously floured surface, roll out the dough into a circle 10 inches in diameter and ½ inch thick. Using a 3-inch round donut cutter, cut out as many donuts as possible. Gather up the donut scraps and repeat rolling and cutting.

4 Carefully lower 2–5 donuts or holes into the hot oil and deep-fry until dark golden, about 1½ minutes. Turn over and cook until dark golden on the second side, about 1 minute longer. Transfer to the towel-lined baking sheet. Repeat to fry the remaining donuts and holes, allowing the oil to return to 360°F between batches.

5 When the donuts and holes are cool enough to handle, roll them in the topping to coat all sides. Serve right away.

2¼ cups all-purpose flour

½ cup granulated sugar

1½ teaspoons baking powder

½ teaspoon salt

1 teaspoon freshly ground pepper

2 large eggs

⅓ cup whole milk

¼ cup extra-virgin olive oil

1½ teaspoons grated lemon zest

Canola or peanut oil for deep-frying

Sugar-and-Spice Topping (page 109)

MAKES ABOUT 10 DONUTS AND THEIR HOLES

MEYER LEMON CUSTARD DONUTS

Meyer lemons have a pure, clear, slightly sweet lemon taste. Their season runs from November through May. If Meyer lemons are unavailable, use a mixture of half Eureka lemons and half oranges when making the glaze and custard.

Canola or peanut oil for brushing and deep-frying

Yeast Donut Dough (page 102)

Meyer Lemon Glaze (page 106)

Meyer Lemon Custard (page 104)

MAKES ABOUT
15 DONUTS

1 Line a baking sheet with waxed paper and brush the paper with oil. Line a second baking sheet with paper towels.

2 Turn the dough out onto a generously floured work surface. Using a floured rolling pin, roll out the dough into a circle about 10 inches in diameter and ½ inch thick. Using a 3-inch round pastry cutter, cut out as many rounds as possible. Use a wide spatula to transfer the donuts to the oiled paper. Gather up the scraps and repeat rolling and cutting. Cover the donuts with a clean kitchen towel and let rise for 30 minutes. The donuts should look soft and puffy, but will not double in size.

3 Pour oil to a depth of 2 inches into a deep-fryer or deep, heavy sauté pan and warm over medium-high heat until it reads 360°F on a deep-frying thermometer. Carefully lower 2–5 donuts into the hot oil and fry until dark golden, about 1½ minutes. Turn over and cook until dark golden on the second side, about 1 minute longer. Transfer to the towel-lined baking sheet. Repeat to fry the remaining donuts, allowing the oil to return to 360°F between batches.

4   When the donuts are cool enough to handle but still warm, dip the tops in the lemon glaze, letting any excess glaze drip back into the bowl. Place on a wire rack and let stand until the glaze sets, about 30 minutes.

5   Fit a pastry bag with a ¼-inch round tip and spoon the custard into the bag. Holding the unglazed bottom and using the tip of a small, sharp knife, cut a small slit in the side of each donut. Press the tip of the pastry bag into the slits and pipe about 1 tablespoon of the lemon custard into each donut. Serve right away.

BAKED CHERRY STREUSEL DONUTS

These round cake donuts have a crisp streusel topping and cakelike interior studded with tangy dried cherries. Unlike most donuts, they are baked in the oven instead of deep-fried, which highlights their fine-crumbed texture. The dough is very soft and must chill for at least an hour to be firm enough to roll.

2 cups all-purpose flour

1½ teaspoons baking powder

¼ teaspoon salt

1 large egg

½ cup granulated sugar

½ cup whole milk

3 tablespoons unsalted butter, melted, plus butter for greasing

1 teaspoon vanilla extract

¼ teaspoon almond extract

¾ cup dried cherries, finely chopped

1 In a bowl, sift together the flour, baking powder, and salt. In a large bowl, using an electric mixer set on low speed (use the paddle attachment for a stand mixer), beat the egg and sugar until creamy and pale. Add the milk, melted butter, and vanilla and almond extracts and beat until well blended. Add the flour mixture and beat, still on low speed, just until the mixture comes together into a soft dough. Stir in the cherries. Cover and refrigerate the dough until firm, at least 1 hour and up to overnight.

2 Preheat the oven to 400°F. Line a baking sheet with parchment paper and butter the paper.

3 Turn the dough out onto a generously floured work surface. Using a floured rolling pin, roll out the dough into a circle about 10 inches in diameter and ½ inch thick. Using a 3-inch round pastry cutter, cut out as many rounds as possible. Gather up the scraps and repeat rolling and cutting.

Using a wide spatula, transfer the donuts to the buttered parchment paper, spacing them about 1½ inches apart. Using a pastry brush, brush the top of each donut with water. Sprinkle the streusel topping evenly over the tops and press gently with your fingertips to help the streusel adhere, if necessary. Bake until the tops are light golden, about 20 minutes. Transfer to a wire rack and let cool slightly.

When the donuts are cool enough to handle, press any bits of streusel that loosened during baking back in place. Using a spoon, drizzle the glaze in a back and forth motion lightly over the top of each donut. Serve right away.

Streusel Topping (page 109)

½ cup Thick Vanilla Glaze (page 107), warmed just until pourable

MAKES ABOUT 10 DONUTS

DULCE DE LECHE DONUTS

Dulce de leche, Spanish for "sweet milk," is a thick, sweet caramel filling or sauce from Central and South America. It is made by slowly cooking sweetened condensed milk until thick and a rich nut brown color—a perfect topping for yeast donuts. Dulce de leche is now available in most markets.

1 In a small saucepan over medium heat, combine the milk and butter. Heat, stirring, until the butter is melted and the mixture is hot but not boiling (about 125°F on an instant-read thermometer). Remove the pan from the heat and set aside.

2 Fit a stand mixer with the paddle attachment. In the mixing bowl, combine 2½ cups of the flour, the brown sugar, cinnamon, salt, and yeast and beat on low speed to mix. Add the hot milk mixture, raise the speed to medium, and beat until well blended. Add the eggs and vanilla and beat until fully incorporated, about 2 minutes. Add the remaining ¾ cup flour and beat until well blended and smooth, about 1 minute longer. The dough will not pull away from the sides of the bowl and will still be somewhat sticky, but your finger should come out clean when you insert it into the center. (For a food processor method, see page 9.)

3 Scrape the dough into a large bowl and cover with a clean kitchen towel. Let the dough stand until well risen and increased in bulk (it may almost double in size), about 45 minutes.

continued on next page →

¾ cup whole milk

3 tablespoons unsalted butter

3¼ cups all-purpose flour

½ cup firmly packed light brown sugar

1 teaspoon ground cinnamon

½ teaspoon salt

1 package (2½ teaspoons) quick-rise yeast

2 large eggs

½ teaspoon vanilla extract

Canola or peanut oil for brushing and deep-frying

1¼ cups purchased dulce de leche

MAKES ABOUT
15 DONUTS AND
THEIR HOLES

4 Line a baking sheet with waxed paper and brush the paper with oil. Line a second baking sheet with paper towels.

5 On a generously floured work surface, roll out the dough into a circle 10 inches in diameter and ½ inch thick. Using a 3-inch round donut cutter, cut out as many donuts as possible. Transfer the donuts and holes to the oiled paper. Gather up the donut scraps and repeat rolling and cutting. (For more information on rolling and cutting, see page 10.) Cover the donuts and holes with a clean kitchen towel and let rise until soft and puffy, about 30 minutes.

6 Pour oil to a depth of 2 inches into a deep-fryer or deep, heavy sauté pan and warm over medium-high heat until it reads 360°F on a deep-frying thermometer. Carefully lower 2–5 donuts or holes into the hot oil and deep-fry until dark golden, about 1½ minutes. Turn over and cook until dark golden on the second side, about 1 minute longer. Transfer to the towel-lined baking sheet. Repeat to fry the remaining donuts and holes, allowing the oil to return to 360°F between batches. (For more information on deep-frying, see page 13.)

7 Using a thin metal spatula, spread a generous tablespoon of dulce de leche over the top of each donut. Spread the tops of the donut holes with about 1 teaspoon dulce de leche, or dip their tops in it. Arrange the donuts and holes on a platter and serve right away.

HONEY-CORNMEAL DONUTS WITH MEYER LEMON GLAZE

Imagine a honey-sweetened corn muffin with a super-crisp crust and you have an idea of what these hearty donuts deliver. Cornmeal adds both a sweet, nutty flavor and a satisfying crunch. The lemon glaze delivers a tart, sweet note.

1 In a bowl, sift together the flour, baking powder, baking soda, and salt. Stir in the cornmeal. In a large bowl, using an electric mixer set on low speed (use the paddle attachment for a stand mixer), beat the butter, granulated sugar, and honey until smooth. Add the egg and egg yolk and beat until well blended. Add half of the flour mixture and beat just until incorporated. Add the buttermilk and 1 teaspoon of the lemon zest and beat until well blended. Add the remaining flour mixture and beat, still on low speed, just until the mixture forms a soft dough.

2 Line a baking sheet with paper towels. Pour oil to a depth of 2 inches into a deep-fryer or deep, heavy sauté pan and warm over medium-high heat until it reads 340°F on a deep-frying thermometer.

continued on next page →

2 cups all-purpose flour

½ teaspoon baking powder

½ teaspoon baking soda

½ teaspoon salt

¾ cup stone-ground cornmeal

2 tablespoons unsalted butter, at room temperature

¼ cup granulated sugar

½ cup honey

1 large egg plus 1 large egg yolk

¼ cup buttermilk

2 teaspoons grated lemon zest

Canola or peanut oil for deep-frying

Meyer Lemon Glaze,
page 106

¼ cup candied violets
or other candied petals,
optional

MAKES ABOUT
12 DONUTS AND
THEIR HOLES

3 On a floured work surface, roll out the dough into a circle 10 inches in diameter and ½ inch thick. Using a 3-inch round donut cutter, cut out as many donuts as possible. Gather up the donut scraps and repeat rolling and cutting. (For more information on rolling and cutting, see page 10.)

4 Carefully lower 2–5 donuts or holes into the hot oil and deep-fry until dark golden, about 1½ minutes. Turn over and cook until dark golden on the second side, about 1 minute longer. Transfer to the towel-lined baking sheet. Repeat to fry the remaining donuts and holes, allowing the oil to return to 340°F between batches. (For more information on deep-frying, see page 13.)

5 When the donuts are cool enough to handle but still warm, dip the tops in the lemon glaze, letting any excess glaze drip back into the bowl. Sprinkle the remaining 1 teaspoon lemon zest evenly over the tops of the donuts and holes, then sprinkle with the candied flowers, if using. Place on a wire rack and let stand until the glaze sets slightly, about 10 minutes. Serve right away.

TRIPLE GINGER DONUTS

The sweet-spicy flavor of ginger is layered in these donuts in three forms: both the grated fresh ginger and the ground spice are mixed into the dough. Chopped crystallized ginger is scattered over the vanilla glaze that tops the finished donuts. A microplane grater is a great tool for grating fresh ginger.

2¼ cups all-purpose flour

2 teaspoons ground ginger

1½ teaspoons baking powder

1 teaspoon ground cinnamon

½ teaspoon salt

2 large eggs

⅔ cup granulated sugar

½ cup whole milk

2 tablespoons unsalted butter, melted

1 teaspoon peeled and finely grated fresh ginger

1 teaspoon vanilla extract

Canola or peanut oil for deep-frying

1 In a bowl, sift together the flour, ground ginger, baking powder, cinnamon, and salt. In a large bowl, using an electric mixer set on low speed (use the paddle attachment for a stand mixer), beat the eggs and sugar until creamy and pale. Add half of the flour mixture and beat just until incorporated. Add the milk, melted butter, fresh ginger, and vanilla and beat until well blended. Add the remaining flour mixture and beat, still on low speed, just until the mixture comes together into a soft dough. Cover and refrigerate the dough until firm, at least 30 minutes and up to 1 hour.

2 Line a baking sheet with paper towels. Pour oil to a depth of 2 inches into a deep-fryer or deep, heavy sauté pan and heat until it reads 360°F on a deep-frying thermometer.

3 On a floured work surface, roll out the dough into a circle 10 inches in diameter and ½ inch thick. Using a 3-inch round donut cutter, cut out as many donuts as possible. Gather up the donut scraps and repeat rolling and cutting. (For more information on rolling and cutting, see page 10.)

Carefully lower 2–5 donuts or holes into the oil and deep-fry until dark golden, about 1½ minutes. Turn over and cook until dark golden on the second side, about 1 minute longer. Transfer to the towel-lined baking sheet. Repeat to fry the remaining donuts and holes, allowing the oil to return to 360°F between batches. (For more information on deep-frying, see page 13.)

Spread the glaze over the top of each donut and hole. Place on a wire rack and let stand until the glaze sets slightly, about 10 minutes. Sprinkle the crystallized ginger over the tops of the donuts and holes and serve right away.

Thick Vanilla Glaze
(page 107)

⅔ cup crystallized ginger,
finely chopped

MAKES ABOUT
10 DONUTS AND
THEIR HOLES

CARAMEL-PECAN DONUTS

These donuts are an example of the delicious practice of mixing salty and sweet ingredients. The recipe uses an easy method of making caramel, which is to simply boil brown sugar, cream, and corn syrup together—the corn syrup keeps the mixture smooth because no sugar crystals will form.

1 In a small saucepan over medium heat, combine the milk and butter and heat, stirring, until the butter melts and the mixture is hot but not boiling (about 125°F on an instant-read thermometer). Remove from the heat.

2 Fit a stand mixer with the paddle attachment. In the mixing bowl, combine 2½ cups of the flour, the brown sugar, cinnamon, salt, and yeast and beat on low speed to mix. Add the hot milk mixture, raise the speed to medium, and beat until well blended and smooth. Add the eggs and vanilla and beat until fully incorporated, about 2 minutes. Add the remaining ¾ cup flour and beat until well blended and smooth, about 1 minute longer. The dough will not pull away from the sides of the bowl and will still be somewhat sticky, but your finger should come out clean when you insert it into the center. (For a food processor method, see page 9.)

3 Scrape the dough into a large bowl and cover the dough with a clean kitchen towel. Let stand until well risen and increased in bulk (it may almost double in size), about 45 minutes.

¾ cup whole milk

3 tablespoons unsalted butter

3¼ cups all-purpose flour

½ cup firmly packed light brown sugar

1 teaspoon ground cinnamon

½ teaspoon salt

1 package (2½ teaspoons) quick-rise yeast

2 large eggs

½ teaspoon vanilla extract

continued on next page →

Canola or peanut oil for brushing and deep-frying

Caramel Glaze (page 108)

1¼ cups pecans, toasted (page 102)

MAKES ABOUT
15 DONUTS AND
THEIR HOLES

4 Line a baking sheet with waxed paper and brush the paper with oil. Line a second baking sheet with paper towels.

5 On a generously floured work surface, roll out the dough into a circle 10 inches in diameter and ½ inch thick. Using a 3-inch round donut cutter, cut out as many donuts as possible. Transfer the donuts and holes to the oiled paper. Gather up the donut scraps and repeat rolling and cutting. (For more information on rolling and cutting, see page 10.) Cover the donuts and holes with a kitchen towel. Let rise until soft and puffy, about 30 minutes.

6 Pour oil to a depth of 2 inches into a deep-fryer or deep, heavy sauté pan and warm over medium-high heat until it reads 360°F on a deep-frying thermometer. Carefully lower 2–5 donuts or holes into the hot oil and deep-fry until dark golden, about 1½ minutes. Turn over and cook until dark golden on the second side, about 1 minute longer. Transfer to the towel-lined baking sheet. Fry the remaining donuts and holes, allowing the oil to return to 360°F between batches. (For more information on deep-frying, see page 13.)

7 Using a thin metal spatula, spread a thin layer of the caramel glaze over the top of each donut. (If the caramel is too thick, heat over low heat until spreadable, 2–3 minutes.) Spread the tops of the donut holes with a thin layer of glaze, or dip their tops in it. Dip the glazed portions of the donuts and holes in the toasted pecans. Press gently with your fingertips to help them adhere, if necessary. Tap the donuts gently to shake off any loose pecan pieces. Serve right away.

BROWN SUGAR DONUTS

The dough for these donuts has an appealing light brown color that deepens into a striking dark golden ring that hints at the orange and spice flavors within. The mix of seasonings—cinnamon, citrus, and caramel-like brown sugar—evokes a hot drink enjoyed by a cozy fire on a cold winter evening.

1 In a small saucepan over medium heat, combine the milk and butter and heat, stirring, until the butter is melted and the mixture is hot but not boiling (125°F on an instant-read thermometer). Remove from the heat.

2 Fit a stand mixer with a paddle attachment. In the mixing bowl, combine 2½ cups of the flour, the brown sugar, cinnamon, salt, and yeast and beat on low speed to mix. Add the hot milk mixture, raise the speed to medium, and beat until well blended. Add the eggs and orange zest and beat until fully incorporated, about 2 minutes. Add the remaining ¾ cup flour and beat until well blended and smooth, about 1 minute longer. The dough will not pull away from the sides of the bowl and will still be somewhat sticky, but your finger should come out clean when you insert it into the center. (For a food processor method, see page 9.)

3 Scrape the dough into a large bowl and cover the dough with a clean kitchen towel. Let stand until the dough is well risen and increased in bulk (it may almost double in size), about 45 minutes.

4 Line a baking sheet with waxed paper and brush the paper with oil. Line a second baking sheet with paper towels.

¾ cup whole milk

3 tablespoons unsalted butter

3¼ cups all-purpose flour

⅓ cup firmly packed light brown sugar

1 teaspoon ground cinnamon

½ teaspoon salt

1 package (2½ teaspoons) quick-rise yeast

2 large eggs

2 teaspoons grated orange zest

continued on next page →

5 On a generously floured work surface, roll out the dough into a circle 10 inches in diameter and ½ inch thick. Using a 2½-inch or 3-inch round donut cutter, cut out as many donuts as possible. Transfer the donuts and holes to the oiled paper. Gather up the donut scraps and repeat rolling and cutting. (For more information on rolling and cutting, see page 10). Cover the donuts and holes with a clean kitchen towel and let rise until soft and puffy, about 30 minutes.

6 Pour oil to a depth of 2 inches into a deep-fryer or deep, heavy sauté pan and warm over medium-high heat until it reads 360°F on a deep-frying thermometer. Carefully lower 3 or 4 donuts or holes into the hot oil and deep-fry until dark golden, about 1½ minutes. Turn over and cook until dark golden on the second side, about 1 minute longer. Transfer to the towel-lined baking sheet. Repeat to fry the remaining donuts and holes, allowing the oil to return to 360°F between batches. (For more information on deep-frying, see page 13.)

7 Using a thin metal spatula, spread about 2 tablespoons of the glaze over the top of each donut. Spread the tops of the donut holes with 1–2 teaspoons of the glaze, or dip their tops in it. Sprinkle with the orange zest and cinnamon-sugar, if using. Let stand until the glaze is slightly set, about 10 minutes. Arrange the donuts and holes on a platter and serve right away.

Canola or peanut oil for brushing and deep-frying

Cinnamon-Orange Glaze (page 106)

¼ cup shredded orange zest, optional

Cinnamon-sugar for sprinkling, optional

MAKES 15–18 DONUTS AND THEIR HOLES

STICKY TOFFEE DONUTS

These donuts are reminiscent of the famed English dessert, sticky toffee pudding. The shiny toffee glaze that covers these donuts makes them a standout in any assortment, as do the chewy bits of dried dates in the dough. The decadent sauce will thicken as it cooks and thicken even more as it cools.

2¼ cups all-purpose flour

1½ teaspoons baking powder

½ teaspoon salt

2 large eggs

⅓ cup firmly packed dark brown sugar

½ cup whole milk

2 tablespoons unsalted butter, melted

1 teaspoon vanilla extract

⅔ cup pitted dates, finely chopped

Canola or peanut oil for deep-frying

Sticky Toffee Glaze (page 108)

½ cup toffee bits

MAKES ABOUT 12 DONUTS AND THEIR HOLES

1 In a bowl, sift together the flour, baking powder, and salt. In a large bowl, using an electric mixer set on low speed (use the paddle attachment for a stand mixer), beat the eggs and brown sugar until creamy. Add half of the flour mixture and beat just until incorporated. Add the milk, melted butter, and vanilla and beat until well blended. Add the remaining flour mixture and beat, still on low speed, just until the mixture comes together into a soft dough. Stir in the dates. Cover and refrigerate the dough until firm, at least 30 minutes and up to 1 hour.

2 Line a large baking sheet with paper towels. Pour oil to a depth of 2 inches into a deep-fryer or deep, heavy sauté pan and warm over medium-high heat until it reads 360°F on a deep-frying thermometer.

3 On a floured work surface, roll out the dough into a circle about 10 inches in diameter and ½ inch thick. Using a 3-inch round donut cutter, cut out as many donuts as possible. Gather up the donut scraps and repeat rolling and cutting. (For more information on rolling and cutting, see page 10.)

4 Carefully lower 2–5 donuts or holes into the hot oil and deep-fry until dark golden, about 1½ minutes. Turn over and cook until dark golden on the second side, about 1 minute longer. Transfer to the towel-lined baking sheet. Repeat to fry the remaining donuts and holes, allowing the oil to return to 360°F between batches. (For more information on deep-frying, see page 13.)

5 When the donuts and holes are cool enough to handle, dip the top half into the glaze, letting any excess drip back into the bowl. Place on a wire rack, sprinkle with the toffee bits, and let stand until slightly set, about 15 minutes. Serve right away.

CHOCOLATE-HAZELNUT FRITTERS

Chocolate and hazelnuts seem to bring out the best in each other. These fritters start with a cocoa powder and hazelnut dough, and then the finished donuts are drizzled with melted chocolate and sprinkled with chopped hazelnuts. To save time, look for skinless hazelnuts in well-stocked markets.

¾ cup plus 2 tablespoons all-purpose flour

¼ cup unsweetened cocoa powder, preferably Dutch process

¼ cup granulated sugar

½ teaspoon baking powder

½ teaspoon salt

½ cup sparkling water

1 large egg, lightly beaten

½ teaspoon vanilla extract

⅔ cup hazelnuts, toasted (page 102) and chopped

Canola or peanut oil for deep-frying

4 oz semisweet chocolate, chopped

MAKES ABOUT 16 FRITTERS

1 In a large bowl, whisk together the flour, cocoa powder, sugar, baking powder, and salt. Make a well in the center of the flour mixture. Add the sparkling water, egg, and vanilla to the well and stir with a fork until well blended. Add ¼ cup of the hazelnuts and stir just until evenly distributed. Set aside.

2 Line a baking sheet with paper towels. Pour oil to a depth of 2 inches into a deep-fryer or deep, heavy sauté pan and warm over medium-high heat until it reads 360°F on a deep-frying thermometer.

3 Using a metal spoon, scoop up a rounded tablespoonful of the batter and drop into the hot oil, or scrape in using a second spoon. Repeat to add 5 or 6 more spoonfuls to the oil. Be sure not to overcrowd the pan. The fritters should float to the top and puff to about double in size. Deep-fry until dark brown and crusty on the first side, about 2 minutes. Using tongs, a wire skimmer, or a slotted spoon, turn and fry until dark brown and crusty on the second side, about 1 minute longer. Transfer to the towel-lined baking sheet to

drain. Repeat to fry the remaining fritters, allowing the oil to return to
360°F between batches.

4 Put the chocolate in the top part of a double boiler and set over
(but not touching) barely simmering water. Heat, stirring often,
until the chocolate melts. Remove from the heat and let cool slightly.
Drizzle about 1 teaspoon of the melted chocolate over each fritter and
let stand for 5 minutes. Put the remaining hazelnuts in a small bowl.
Dip the chocolate-coated portions of the fritters in the nuts and serve.

BANANA CREAM DONUTS

These custard-filled treats are like a taste of banana cream pie in a donut. A light vanilla glaze doubles the decadence. For an indulgent, dessert-worthy finish, top the donuts with whipped cream, sliced bananas, a drizzle of caramel glaze (page 108), and a sprinkle of cinnamon-sugar.

Canola or peanut oil for brushing and deep-frying

Yeast Donut Dough (page 102)

Vanilla Glaze (page 107)

Banana Custard (page 104)

MAKES ABOUT 15 DONUTS

1 Line a baking sheet with waxed paper and brush the paper with oil. Line a second baking sheet with paper towels.

2 Turn the dough out onto a generously floured work surface. Using a floured rolling pin, roll out the dough into a circle about 10 inches in diameter and ½ inch thick. Using a 3-inch round pastry cutter, cut out as many rounds as possible. Use a wide spatula to transfer the donuts to the oiled paper. Gather up the scraps and repeat rolling and cutting. Cover the donuts with a clean kitchen towel and let rise for 30 minutes. The donuts should look soft and puffy, but will not double in size.

3 Pour oil to a depth of 2 inches into a deep-fryer or deep, heavy sauté pan and warm over medium-high heat until it reads 360°F on a deep-frying thermometer. Carefully lower 2–5 donuts into the hot oil and fry until dark golden in color, about 1½ minutes. Turn over and cook until dark golden in color on the second side, about 1 minute longer. Transfer to the towel-lined baking sheet. Repeat to fry the remaining donuts, allowing the oil to return to 360°F between batches. (For more information on deep-frying, see page 13.)

4 When the donuts are cool enough to handle but still warm, dip all sides in the vanilla glaze, letting any excess glaze drip back into the bowl. Place on a wire rack and let stand until the glaze sets, about 30 minutes.

5 Fit a pastry bag with a ¼-inch round tip and spoon the custard into the bag. Holding the bottom and using the tip of a small, sharp knife, cut a ½-inch slit in the side of each donut. Press the tip into the slit and pipe 1 tablespoon of the custard into each donut. Serve right away.

CHOCOLATE-PEPPERMINT CRUNCH DONUTS

Soft and crunchy, chocolatey and nutty: these donuts have it all. Cocoa powder adds deep chocolate flavor and color to these uniquely shaped treats, while crushed peppermint candies contribute a sweet, crispy topping.

1 In a small saucepan over medium heat, combine the milk and butter. Heat, stirring, until the butter is melted and the mixture is hot but not boiling (about 125°F on an instant-read thermometer). Remove from the heat. Set aside.

2 Fit a stand mixer with the paddle attachment. In the mixing bowl, combine 2½ cups of the flour, the cocoa powder, sugar, salt, and yeast and beat on low speed to mix. Add the hot milk mixture, raise the speed to medium, and beat until well blended. Add the eggs and vanilla and beat until incorporated, about 2 minutes. Add the remaining ½ cup flour and beat until well blended and smooth, about 1 minute longer. The dough will not pull away from the sides of the bowl and will still be somewhat sticky, but your finger should come out clean when you insert it into the center. (For a food processor method, see page 9.)

3 Scrape the dough into a large bowl and cover with a clean kitchen towel. Let stand until the dough is well risen and increased in bulk (it may almost double in size), about 45 minutes.

¾ cup whole milk

3 tablespoons unsalted butter

3 cups all-purpose flour

¼ cup unsweetened cocoa powder, preferably Dutch process

⅓ cup granulated sugar

½ teaspoon salt

1 package (2½ teaspoons) quick-rise yeast

2 large eggs

½ teaspoon vanilla extract

Canola or peanut oil for brushing and deep-frying

continued on next page →

Chocolate Glaze
(page 108)

1 cup crushed
peppermint candies

MAKES ABOUT
16 DONUTS AND
THEIR HOLES

4 Line a baking sheet with waxed paper and brush the paper with oil. Line a second baking sheet with paper towels.

5 On a floured work surface, roll out the dough into a 12-by-12-inch square. Using a long knife, cut the dough into sixteen 3-inch squares. Using a paring knife, cut out 1-inch square holes. Transfer the donuts and holes to the oiled paper. Gather up the donut scraps and repeat rolling and cutting. (To make round donuts, follow the instructions for rolling and cutting on page 10.) Cover the donuts and holes with a clean kitchen towel and let rise until soft and puffy, about 30 minutes.

6 Pour oil to a depth of 2 inches into a deep-fryer or deep, heavy sauté pan and warm over medium-high heat until it reads 350°F on a deep-frying thermometer. Carefully lower 2–5 donuts or holes into the hot oil and deep-fry until dark brown and crusty on the first side, about 1½ minutes. Turn over and cook until dark brown and crusty on the second side, about 1 minute longer. Transfer to the towel-lined baking sheet. Repeat to fry the remaining donuts and holes, allowing the oil to return to 350°F between batches. (For more information on deep-frying, see page 13.)

7 When the donuts and holes are cool enough to handle, dip the tops in the chocolate glaze, letting any excess glaze drip back into the bowl. (You may not use all of the glaze, but this makes for easier dipping.) Place on a wire rack and let stand until the glaze sets slightly, about 10 minutes. Sprinkle a generous tablespoon of the crushed peppermints over the top of each donut, pressing gently on the candy to help it adhere. Arrange on a platter and serve right away.

MAPLE-BACON DONUTS

These crowd-pleasing donuts feature a maple glaze adorned with crisp pieces of bacon. The bacon is dipped into maple syrup before it's baked, raising the bar on the favorite sweet-and-salty combination to new heights.

1 Preheat the oven to 375°F. Line a large rimmed baking sheet with aluminum foil. Line a plate with paper towels.

2 Pour the maple syrup into a shallow bowl and dip the bacon slices in the syrup to coat on all sides. Arrange the slices on the baking sheet, laying them flat and placing them at least 1 inch apart. Bake until the bacon is browned and crisp, about 20 minutes. Remove from the oven and transfer to the towel-lined plate to drain. Blot the tops with additional paper towels. The bacon will get crisper as it cools. When cool, break or cut the bacon into ¼–½-inch pieces. Set aside.

3 In a bowl, sift together the flour, baking powder, and salt. In a large bowl, using an electric mixer set on low speed (use the paddle attachment for a stand mixer), beat the eggs, granulated sugar, and brown sugar until creamy. Add half of the flour mixture and beat just until incorporated. Add the milk, melted butter, and vanilla and beat until well blended. Add the remaining flour mixture and beat, still on low speed, just until the mixture comes together into a soft dough. Cover and refrigerate the dough until firm, at least 30 minutes and up to 1 hour.

¼ cup maple syrup

5 strips thinly sliced bacon

2¼ cups all-purpose flour

1½ teaspoons baking powder

½ teaspoon salt

2 large eggs

¼ cup granulated sugar

¼ cup firmly packed brown sugar

½ cup whole milk

2 tablespoons unsalted butter, melted

1 teaspoon vanilla extract

Canola or peanut oil for deep-frying

Maple Glaze (page 108)

MAKES ABOUT 10 DONUTS AND THEIR HOLES

continued on next page ⟶

4 Line a baking sheet with paper towels. Pour oil to a depth of 2 inches into a deep-fryer or deep, heavy sauté pan and warm over medium-high heat until it reads 360°F on a deep-frying thermometer.

5 On a floured work surface, roll out the dough into a circle 10 inches in diameter and ½ inch thick. Using a 3-inch round donut cutter, cut out as many donuts as possible. Gather up the donut scraps and repeat rolling and cutting. (For more information on rolling and cutting, see page 10.)

6 Carefully lower 2–5 donuts or holes into the oil and deep-fry until dark golden, about 1½ minutes. Turn over and cook until dark golden on the second side, about 1 minute longer. Transfer to the towel-lined baking sheet. Repeat to fry the remaining donuts and holes, allowing the oil to return to 360°F between batches. (For more information on deep-frying, see page 13.)

7 Using a thin metal spatula, spread about 2 tablespoons of the maple glaze over the top of each donut. Spread the tops of the donut holes with 1–2 teaspoons of the glaze, or dip their tops in it. Sprinkle the bacon pieces over the glazed portions of the donuts and donut holes and press gently with your fingertips to help them adhere, if necessary. Arrange the donuts and their holes on a platter and serve right away.

CHOCOLATE-CHILE DONUTS

Ancho chile powder has a deep flavor and a subtle heat that marries well with chocolate, and likewise these chocolate donuts. If desired, you can increase the amount of chile powder to suit your taste, but take care that the chiles do not overpower the chocolate and create nothing but a hot, spicy result.

1 cup all-purpose flour

1 cup cake flour

¼ cup unsweetened cocoa powder, preferably Dutch process

1 teaspoon baking powder

½ teaspoon baking soda

½ teaspoon salt

1 large egg

½ cup granulated sugar

½ cup buttermilk

1 tablespoon unsalted butter, melted

2¼ teaspoons ancho chile powder

1 teaspoon vanilla extract

Canola or peanut oil for deep-frying

1 In a bowl, sift together the flours, cocoa powder, baking powder, baking soda, and salt. In a large bowl, using an electric mixer set on low speed (use the paddle attachment for a stand mixer), beat the egg and sugar until creamy and pale. Add the buttermilk, melted butter, 1½ teaspoons of the chile powder, and the vanilla and beat until blended. Add the flour mixture and beat, still on low speed, just until the mixture comes together into a soft dough. Cover and refrigerate the dough until firm, at least 30 minutes and up to 1 hour.

2 Line a baking sheet with paper towels. Pour oil to a depth of 2 inches into a deep-fryer or deep, heavy-bottomed sauté pan and warm over medium-high heat until it reads 360°F on a deep-frying thermometer.

3 On a generously floured work surface, roll out the dough into a circle 10 inches in diameter and ½ inch thick. Using a 3-inch round donut cutter, cut out as many donuts as possible. Gather up the donut scraps and repeat rolling and cutting. (For more information on rolling and cutting, see page 10.)

4 Carefully lower 2–5 donuts or holes into the hot oil and deep-fry until dark brown and crusty on the first side, about 1½ minutes.

Turn over and cook until dark brown and crusty on the second side, about 1 minute longer. Transfer to the towel-lined baking sheet. Repeat to fry the remaining donuts and holes, allowing the oil to return to 360°F between batches.

5 Stir ½ teaspoon of the remaining chile powder into the chocolate glaze. When the donuts are cool enough to handle, dip the tops in the glaze, then sprinkle with the remaining ¼ teaspoon chile powder and the pepitas, if using. Let the glaze set for 10 minutes. Serve right away.

Chocolate Glaze
(page 108)

½ cup pepitas (pumpkin seeds), optional

MAKES ABOUT
10 DONUTS AND
THEIR HOLES

DOUBLE-DIPPED CHOCOLATE DONUTS

Chocolate yeast-raised donuts frosted with a layer of bittersweet chocolate ganache make a sophisticated party treat. Double-dipping the donuts in the chocolate mixture produces the thick topping. For a special treat, top each donut with a scoop of raspberry gelato, chocolate sauce, and colorful sprinkles.

1 In a small saucepan over medium heat, combine the milk and butter and heat, stirring, until the butter melts and the mixture is hot but not boiling (about 125°F on an instant-read thermometer). Remove from the heat. Set aside.

2 Fit a stand mixer with the paddle attachment. In the mixing bowl, combine 2½ cups of the flour, the cocoa powder, sugar, salt, and yeast and beat on low speed to mix. Add the hot milk mixture, raise the speed to medium, and beat until well blended. Add the eggs and vanilla and beat until incorporated, about 2 minutes. Add the remaining ½ cup flour and beat until well blended and smooth, about 1 minute longer. The dough will not pull away from the sides of the bowl and will still be somewhat sticky, but your finger should come out clean when you insert it into the center. (For a food processor method, see page 9.)

3 Scrape the dough into a large bowl and cover with a kitchen towel. Let the dough stand until well risen and increased in bulk (it may almost double in size), about 45 minutes.

¾ cup whole milk

3 tablespoons unsalted butter

3 cups all-purpose flour

¼ cup unsweetened cocoa powder, preferably Dutch process

⅓ cup granulated sugar

½ teaspoon salt

1 package (2½ teaspoons) quick-rise yeast

2 large eggs

½ teaspoon vanilla extract

continued on next page →

Canola or peanut oil for brushing and deep-frying

Chocolate Ganache
(page 106)

MAKES ABOUT
15 DONUTS AND
THEIR HOLES

4 Line a baking sheet with waxed paper and brush the paper with oil. Line a second baking sheet with paper towels.

5 On a generously floured work surface, roll out the dough into a circle 10 inches in diameter and ½ inch thick. Using a 3-inch round donut cutter, cut out as many donuts as possible. Transfer the donuts and holes to the oiled paper. Gather up the donut scraps and repeat rolling and cutting. (For more information on rolling and cutting, see page 10.) Cover the donuts and holes with a clean kitchen towel and let rise until soft and puffy, about 30 minutes.

6 Pour oil to a depth of 2 inches into a deep-fryer or deep, heavy sauté pan and warm over medium-high heat until it reads 360°F on a deep-frying thermometer. Carefully lower 2–5 donuts or holes into the hot oil and deep-fry until dark brown and crusty on the first side, about 1½ minutes. Turn over and cook until dark brown and crusty on the second side, about 1 minute longer. Transfer to the towel-lined baking sheet. Repeat to fry the remaining donuts and holes, allowing the oil to return to 360°F between batches. (For more information on deep-frying, see page 13.)

7 If the ganache seems too thick for dipping, transfer it to a stainless-steel bowl and set over (but not touching) a saucepan of simmering water. Heat, stirring until smooth. When the donuts and donut holes are cool enough to handle, dip the tops in the ganache, letting any excess drip back into the bowl. Place on a wire rack and let stand until the ganache sets slightly, about 10 minutes, then dip a second time. Serve right away.

LEMON-FILLED BEIGNETS

Beignets, a beloved deep-fried but light and airy pastry creation from France, can be made from a yeast dough; a thick batter; or a pâte à choux, or cream puff, dough. Lemon curd is called for here, but traditional beignets can also contain any flavor of jam, such as strawberry or blueberry.

⅔ cup whole milk

2¼ cups all-purpose flour

⅓ cup granulated sugar

¼ teaspoon salt

1 package (2½ teaspoons) quick-rise yeast

6 tablespoons unsalted butter, at room temperature

1 large egg plus 1 large egg yolk

1 teaspoon grated lemon zest

½ teaspoon vanilla extract

Canola or peanut oil for brushing and deep-frying

1 In a small saucepan over medium heat, warm the milk until hot but not boiling (about 125°F on an instant-read thermometer). Remove the pan from the heat.

2 Fit a stand mixer with the paddle attachment. In the mixing bowl, combine the flour, granulated sugar, salt, and yeast and beat on low speed to mix. Add the hot milk, raise the speed to medium, and beat until blended. Add the butter, whole egg and egg yolk, lemon zest, and vanilla and beat until well blended and smooth, about 2 minutes. The dough will not pull away from the sides of the bowl and will still be somewhat sticky, but your finger should come out clean when you insert it into the center. (For a food processor method, see page 9.) Scrape the dough into a large bowl, cover, and let rest for about 10 minutes.

3 Line a baking sheet with waxed paper and brush the paper with oil. Line a second baking sheet with paper towels.

4 Lightly grease the palms of your hands with oil. Pull off about 1 teaspoon of the dough and roll it between your palms into a smooth ball, then press into a disk about 2 inches in diameter. Place

continued on next page ⟶

on the oiled paper. Spoon about 1 teaspoonful of the lemon curd into the center of the dough disk. Make a second dough disk the same way and place on top of the first, stretching the edges over the curd. Pinch the edges to seal tightly. Repeat with the remaining dough and lemon curd. You should have about 18 beignets. Cover with a clean kitchen towel and let rise for 30 minutes. The beignets should look soft and puffy, but will not double in size.

5 Pour oil to a depth of 2 inches into a deep-fryer or deep, heavy sauté pan and warm over medium-high heat until it reads 365°F on a deep-frying thermometer.

6 Using a spatula, one at a time, transfer 4–5 beignets from the baking sheet to the hot oil, sliding them in gently. Be sure not to overcrowd the pan. The beignets should float to the top and puff to about double their size. Deep-fry until dark golden on the first side, about 1½ minutes. Using tongs, turn and fry until dark golden on the second side, about 1½ minutes longer. Transfer to the towel-lined baking sheet to drain. Repeat to fry the remaining beignets, allowing the oil to return to 365°F between batches. (For more information on deep-frying, see page 13.)

7 Arrange the beignets on a platter. Using a fine-mesh sieve, dust with confectioners' sugar and serve right away.

6 tablespoons store-bought lemon curd

Confectioners' sugar for dusting

MAKES ABOUT 18 BEIGNETS

ESPRESSO-GLAZED DONUTS

Coffee and donuts may be one of the all-time favorite classic combinations, but these dark beauties take the popular duo a step higher by gilding the donuts themselves with a bold espresso glaze. A warm cup of espresso or cappuccino makes the perfect accompaniment.

Canola or peanut oil for brushing and deep frying

Yeast Donut Dough (page 102)

Espresso Glaze (page 109)

MAKES ABOUT 15 DONUTS AND THEIR HOLES

1 Line a baking sheet with waxed paper and brush the paper with oil. Line a second baking sheet with paper towels.

2 On a generously floured work surface, roll out the dough into a circle 10 inches in diameter and ½ inch thick. Using a 3-inch round donut cutter, cut out as many donuts as possible. Transfer the donuts and holes to the oiled paper. Gather up the donut scraps and repeat rolling and cutting. (For more information on rolling and cutting, see page 10.) Cover the donuts and holes with a clean kitchen towel and let rise until soft and puffy, about 30 minutes.

3 Pour oil to a depth of 2 inches into a deep-fryer or deep, heavy sauté pan and warm over medium-high heat until it reads 360°F on a deep-frying thermometer. Carefully lower 2–5 donuts or holes into the hot oil and deep-fry until dark golden, about 1½ minutes. Turn over and cook until dark golden on the second side, about 1 minute longer. Transfer to the towel-lined baking sheet. Repeat to fry the remaining donuts and holes, allowing the oil to return to 360°F between batches. (For more information on deep-frying, see page 13.)

4 Using a thin metal spatula, spread about 2 tablespoons of the glaze over the top of each donut. Spread the tops of the donut holes with 1–2 teaspoons of the glaze, or dip their tops in it. Let the glaze set for 10 minutes. Arrange the donuts and holes on a platter and serve right away.

CARDAMOM-HONEY BALLS

These super-moist, syrup-soaked, bite-sized donuts get even better after standing overnight. In India they are known as *gulab jamun*, distinguished by a dough that has equal parts flour and dry milk powder. Rose water, available in specialty-foods markets, adds a heady floral scent to the syrup.

½ cup all-purpose flour

½ cup nonfat dry milk powder

⅛ teaspoon baking soda

¼ teaspoon salt

2 tablespoons unsalted butter, melted

¼ cup whole milk

Canola or peanut oil for brushing and deep-frying

1 In a large bowl, whisk together the flour, milk powder, baking soda, and salt. Using a large spoon, stir in the melted butter just until evenly moist and fine crumbs form. Add the whole milk and stir just until the mixture comes together into a soft dough. Cover and let rest for 10 minutes (any remaining streaks of flour and milk powder will be absorbed during resting).

2 Line a baking sheet with waxed paper and brush the paper with oil. Line a second baking sheet with paper towels. Pour oil to a depth of 2 inches into a deep-fryer or deep, heavy sauté pan and warm over medium-high heat until it reads 350°F on a deep-frying thermometer.

3 Lightly grease the palms of your hands with oil. Pull off about 1 tablespoon of the dough and roll it between your palms into a smooth ball about 1 inch in diameter. Place it on the oiled paper. Repeat to shape the remaining dough, spacing the balls 1–2 inches apart on the baking sheet. You should have 18 balls.

4 Using a slotted spoon, one or two at a time, transfer 5–6 donut balls from the baking sheet to the hot oil, sliding them in gently.

The donut balls should float to the top and increase in size. Deep-fry until dark golden on all sides, using the slotted spoon to roll them as needed to cook them evenly, about 3½ minutes total. Transfer to the towel-lined baking sheet to drain. Repeat to fry the remaining donut balls, allowing the oil to return to 350°F between batches.

5 To make the spiced syrup, in a saucepan over medium heat, combine 1 cup water, the sugar, honey, cardamom, and saffron and bring to a boil, stirring to dissolve the sugar. Cook, stirring often, for 1 minute. Pour into a heatproof bowl and stir in the rose water. Keep warm.

6 When all the donut balls are fried, transfer them to the pan of warm syrup and stir gently to coat. Let stand in the syrup at room temperature for at least 2 hours. Or, cover, refrigerate, and let the balls stand in the syrup up to overnight.

7 To serve, place 3 donut balls into each of 6 small bowls and spoon the syrup over them. Sprinkle with the pistachios and serve cold or at room temperature.

SPICED SYRUP

1 cup granulated sugar

¼ cup honey

¼ teaspoon ground cardamom

Pinch of saffron

1 teaspoon rose water

¼ cup chopped shelled unsalted pistachios

MAKES ABOUT 18 DONUT BALLS

CHURROS WITH CHOCOLATE SAUCE

The long, ridged horns of the Churro breed of Spanish sheep inspired the elongated shape of the well-loved Latin American donuts called churros. Made by piping strips of pâte à choux (a classic pastry borrowed from France) into hot oil, they are often served with cups of warm chocolate sauce for dipping.

1 To make the chocolate sauce, in a saucepan over medium-low heat, combine the half-and-half, butter, cocoa powder, and sugar and bring to a simmer, whisking to dissolve the sugar and cocoa powder. Cook for 1 minute, whisking constantly. Remove from the heat and stir in the vanilla. Pour the sauce into a heatproof bowl. Set aside and cover to keep warm.

2 To make the churros, in a saucepan over medium heat, combine 1 cup water, the butter, and salt and bring to a boil, stirring to melt the butter. Add the flour all at once and stir vigorously with a wooden spoon until the flour is incorporated and the dough pulls away from the sides of the pan in a ball. Reduce the heat to low and cook, stirring constantly, for 1 minute. The dough will continue to pull away from the pan sides in a large clump.

3 Scrape the dough into a large bowl. Using an electric mixer set on medium speed (use the paddle attachment for a stand mixer),

continued on next page →

CHOCOLATE SAUCE

1 cup half-and-half

3 tablespoons unsalted butter, cut into ½-inch cubes

⅓ cup unsweetened cocoa, preferably Dutch process

½ cup granulated sugar

1 teaspoon vanilla extract

CHURROS

½ cup unsalted butter

½ teaspoon salt

1 cup all-purpose flour

3 large eggs, at room temperature

½ teaspoon vanilla extract

Canola oil for deep-frying

⅔ cup granulated sugar

1 teaspoon ground cinnamon

MAKES ABOUT
35 CHURROS

beat until the dough forms large clumps, about 1 minute. Add the eggs one at a time, beating until smooth after each addition. Beat in the vanilla.

4 Line a baking sheet with paper towels. Pour oil to a depth of 2 inches into a deep-fryer or deep, heavy sauté pan and warm over medium-high heat until it reads 360°F on a deep-frying thermometer.

5 Fit a pastry bag with a ½-inch star tip and spoon the dough into the bag. Dip a large, wide spatula into the hot oil, letting any excess drip back into the fryer. Pipe 2 dough strips, each 6–7 inches long, onto the spatula, spacing them about 1 inch apart. Slide the spatula into the hot oil and let the dough slide off into the oil. Repeat to add 2–4 more strips to the oil. Be sure not to overcrowd the pan. The churros should float to the top and increase in size. Deep-fry until dark golden on the first side, about 2 minutes. Using tongs, a wire skimmer, or a slotted spoon, turn and fry until dark golden on the second side, about 1½ minutes longer. Transfer to the towel-lined baking sheet to drain. Repeat to fry the remaining churros, allowing the oil to return to 360°F between batches. (For more information on deep-frying, see page 13.)

6 In a large, shallow bowl, mix together the sugar and cinnamon. When the churros are cool enough to handle, roll them in the cinnamon-sugar to coat generously. (You may have extra cinnamon-sugar, but this makes for easier coating.) Arrange the churros on a platter and serve right away with the warm chocolate sauce for dipping.

RICOTTA ZEPPOLE

Italian zeppole are famously light in texture. Each year on March 19, zeppole are cooked all over Italy to celebrate the feast of Saint Joseph, who answered prayers to end a severe drought during the Middle Ages, and who also reportedly had a way with fritters.

1 Line a large baking sheet with paper towels. Pour oil to a depth of 2 inches into a deep-fryer or deep, heavy sauté pan and warm over medium-high heat until it reads 360°F on a deep-frying thermometer.

2 In a large bowl, whisk together the eggs, granulated sugar, and vanilla until well blended. Add the orange zest and ricotta and whisk to combine. Using a large spoon, stir in the flour, baking powder, and salt and mix just until smoothly incorporated.

3 Using a metal spoon, scoop up a tablespoonful of the batter and drop gently into the hot oil. Repeat to add 3–5 more spoonfuls to the oil. Do not overcrowd the pan. The zeppole should float to the top and puff to about double their size. Deep-fry until dark golden on the first side, about 1 minute. Using tongs, a wire skimmer, or a slotted spoon, turn and fry until dark golden on the second side, about 1 minute longer. Transfer to the towel-lined baking sheet to drain. Repeat to fry the remaining zeppole, allowing the oil to return to 360°F between batches.

4 Arrange the zeppole on a platter. Using a fine-mesh sieve, dust with confectioners' sugar and orange zest. Serve right away.

Canola or peanut oil for deep-frying

3 large eggs

⅓ cup granulated sugar

½ teaspoon vanilla extract

1 teaspoon grated orange zest, plus extra for garnishing

1 cup whole-milk ricotta cheese

1¼ cups all-purpose flour

1 teaspoon baking powder

¼ teaspoon salt

Confectioners' sugar for dusting

MAKES ABOUT 28 ZEPPOLE

BOMBOLINI

Bombolini are bite-sized, jam-filled donuts made from a traditional pâte à choux (cream-puff dough). They resemble small, light jelly donuts that, as the name suggests, explode in your mouth like a tiny, sweet bomb. Be sure to use a smooth jam or one with fruit pieces small enough to fit through the piping tip.

1 cup whole milk

½ cup unsalted butter, cut into ½-inch cubes

½ teaspoon salt

1 cup all-purpose flour

3 large eggs, at room temperature

½ teaspoon vanilla extract

Canola or peanut oil for deep-frying

½ cup granulated sugar

¾ cup best-quality cherry, apricot, or plum jam

MAKES ABOUT 30 BOMBOLINI

1 In a saucepan over medium heat, combine the milk, butter, and salt and bring to a boil, stirring to melt the butter. Add the flour all at once and stir vigorously with a wooden spoon until the flour is incorporated and the dough pulls away from the sides of the pan in a ball. Reduce the heat to low and cook, stirring constantly, for 1 minute.

2 Scrape the dough into a large bowl. Using an electric mixer set on medium speed (use the paddle attachment for a stand mixer), beat until the dough forms large clumps, about 1 minute. Add the eggs one at a time, beating until smooth after each addition. Beat in the vanilla. Cover and refrigerate the dough until firm, about 1 hour.

3 Line a baking sheet with paper towels. Pour oil to a depth of 2 inches into a deep-fryer or deep, heavy sauté pan and warm over medium-high heat until it reads 360°F on a deep-frying thermometer. Using a 1-tablespoon ice cream scoop, scoop up a round of dough and drop into the hot oil. Repeat to add 3–5 more rounds to the oil. Deep-fry until golden on the first side, about 2 minutes. Turn and fry until golden on the second side, about 1½ minutes longer. Transfer

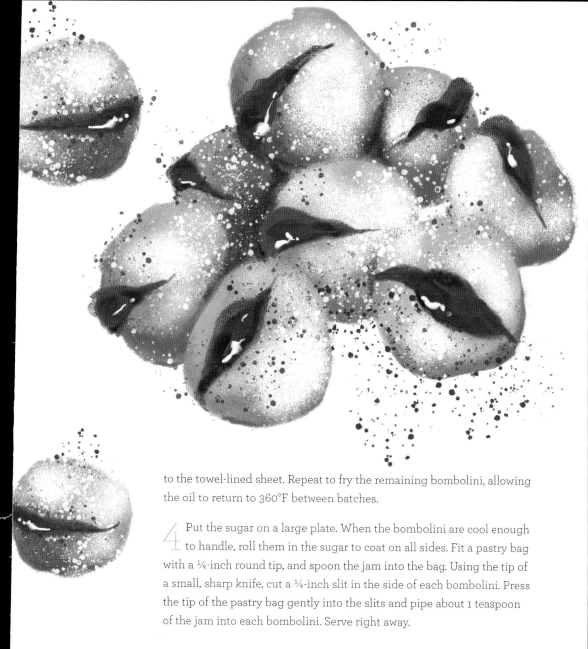

to the towel-lined sheet. Repeat to fry the remaining bombolini, allowing the oil to return to 360°F between batches.

4 Put the sugar on a large plate. When the bombolini are cool enough to handle, roll them in the sugar to coat on all sides. Fit a pastry bag with a ¼-inch round tip, and spoon the jam into the bag. Using the tip of a small, sharp knife, cut a ¼-inch slit in the side of each bombolini. Press the tip of the pastry bag gently into the slits and pipe about 1 teaspoon of the jam into each bombolini. Serve right away.

CHOCOLATE-GLAZED FRENCH CRULLERS

French crullers, identified by their famous fluted rings, have a light and airy texture produced by their age-old pâte à choux, which uses only flour, butter, water, and eggs. Chocolate glaze is used here, but cinnamon, vanilla, or maple glaze (see pages 107 and 108) also make delectable options.

1 In a saucepan over medium heat, combine ½ cup water, the butter, sugar, and salt and bring to a boil, stirring to melt the butter. Add the flour all at once and stir vigorously with a wooden spoon until the flour is incorporated and the dough pulls away from the sides of the pan in a ball. Reduce the heat to low and cook, stirring constantly, for 1 minute. The dough will continue to pull away from the pan sides in a large clump.

2 Scrape the dough into a large bowl. Using an electric mixer set on medium speed (use the paddle attachment for a stand mixer), beat until the dough forms large clumps, about 1 minute. Add the eggs one at a time, beating until smoothly blended after each addition. Add the vanilla and beat until smooth.

3 Pour oil to a depth of 2 inches into a deep-fryer or deep, heavy sauté pan and warm over medium-high heat until it reads 360°F on a deep-frying thermometer.

4 tablespoons unsalted butter, cut into small pieces

½ teaspoon granulated sugar

½ teaspoon salt

½ cup all-purpose flour

2 large eggs, at room temperature

½ teaspoon vanilla extract

Canola or peanut oil for brushing and deep-frying

⅔ cup Chocolate Glaze (page 108)

MAKES 8 CRULLERS

continued on next page →

4 Line a baking sheet with paper towels. Line a second baking sheet with waxed paper. Cut eight 4-inch squares of waxed paper and arrange them on the paper-lined baking sheet. Brush the paper squares with oil. Fit a pastry bag with a ½-inch star tip and fill the bag with the dough. Pipe a 3-inch circle of dough onto each of the 8 squares of paper.

5 When the oil is hot, carefully turn over one of the dough-topped paper pieces and slide the dough circle into the hot oil. Repeat to add 1 or 2 more dough circles to the oil. Be sure not to overcrowd the pan. The crullers should increase in size. Deep-fry until dark golden on the first side, about 2 minutes. Using tongs, a wire skimmer, or a slotted spoon, turn and fry until dark golden on the second side, about 1½ minutes longer. Transfer to the towel-lined baking sheet, fluted side up, to drain. Repeat to fry the remaining crullers, allowing the oil to return to 360°F between batches. (For more information on deep-frying, see page 13.)

6 Using a spoon or a small squeeze bottle filled with the glaze, drizzle the glaze in a back-and-forth pattern over the top of each cruller. Let the glaze set for 10 minutes. Arrange on a platter and serve right away.

CREOLE CALAS

In the early twentieth century, the morning calls of "*Bella calas, tout chaud!*" ("Beautiful hot calas!") could be heard on the streets of New Orleans. These rice fritters were sold by African-American women from baskets balanced on their heads. The calas sellers are now gone, but the popular recipe lives on.

1 In a large bowl, whisk together the flour, brown sugar, baking powder, salt, and nutmeg. Using a large spoon, stir in the eggs and vanilla. Stir in the rice just until evenly distributed. Cover and let rest for 10 minutes.

2 Line a baking sheet with paper towels. Pour oil to a depth of 2 inches into a deep-fryer or deep, heavy sauté pan and warm over medium-high heat until it reads 360°F on a deep-frying thermometer.

3 Using a metal spoon, scoop up a rounded tablespoonful of the batter and drop into the hot oil. Repeat to add 5 or 6 spoonfuls to the oil. The calas should float to the top and puff to about double their size. Deep-fry until dark golden on the first side, about 1½ minutes. Using tongs, a wire skimmer, or a slotted spoon, turn and fry until dark golden on the second side, about 1 minute longer. (The thick batter will produce slightly flattened fritters.) Transfer to the towel-lined baking sheet to drain. Repeat to fry the remaining calas, allowing the oil to return to 360°F between batches.

4 Arrange the calas on a platter. Using a fine-mesh sieve, dust with confectioners' sugar. Serve right away, accompanied by the jam.

½ cup all-purpose flour

¼ cup firmly packed light brown sugar

1½ teaspoons baking powder

¼ teaspoon salt

⅛ teaspoon freshly grated nutmeg

2 large eggs, lightly beaten

1 teaspoon vanilla extract

2 cups cooked white rice

Canola or peanut oil for deep-frying

Confectioners' sugar for dusting

Cherry, blueberry, or raspberry jam for serving

MAKES ABOUT 30 CALAS

basic recipes and techniques

YEAST DONUT DOUGH

¾ cup whole milk

3 tablespoons unsalted butter

3¼ cups all-purpose flour

⅓ cup granulated sugar

½ teaspoon salt

1 package (2½ teaspoons) quick-rise yeast

2 large eggs

½ teaspoon vanilla extract

MAKES ONE 10-INCH DOUGH ROUND

In a small saucepan over medium heat, combine the milk and butter and heat, stirring, until the butter is melted and the mixture is hot but not boiling (about 125°F on an instant-read thermometer). Remove from the heat.

Fit a stand mixer with the paddle attachment. In the mixing bowl, combine 2½ cups of the flour, the sugar, salt, and yeast and beat on low speed to mix. Add the hot milk mixture, raise the speed to medium, and beat until well blended. Add the eggs and vanilla and beat until fully incorporated, about 2 minutes. Add the remaining ¾ cup flour and beat until the dough is well blended and smooth, about 1 minute longer. The dough will not pull away from the sides of the bowl and will still be somewhat sticky. (If you don't have a stand mixer, turn to page 9 for a food processor method.)

Scrape the dough into a large bowl and cover with a clean kitchen towel. Let stand in a warm place until well risen and increased in bulk (it may almost double in size), about 45 minutes. Use the dough right away, as directed in the recipe.

TOASTING COCONUT

Preheat the oven to 325°F. Spread shredded dried coconut in a single layer in a large rimmed baking sheet. Bake, stirring occasionally for even browning, until the coconut is fragrant and the color deepens, about 5–10 minutes. Transfer to a plate to cool.

TOASTING NUTS

ON THE STOVETOP Spread the nuts in an even layer in a small sauté pan. Toast the nuts over medium heat, stirring often, until fragrant and lightly browned, about 10–15 minutes. Transfer to a plate to cool.

IN THE OVEN Preheat the oven to 325°F. Spread the nuts in an even layer in a large rimmed baking sheet. Bake, stirring occasionally for even browning, until the nuts are fragrant and lightly browned, about 10–15 minutes. Transfer to a plate to cool.

fillings, glazes, and toppings

MEYER LEMON CUSTARD

1 cup whole milk

3 large egg yolks

½ cup granulated sugar

4 teaspoons cornstarch

2 tablespoons unsalted butter, at room temperature

½ teaspoon grated Meyer lemon zest

¼ cup fresh Meyer lemon juice

1 teaspoon vanilla extract

MAKES ABOUT 1½ CUPS

In a saucepan over medium heat, warm the milk until small bubbles appear around the edges of the pan. Remove from the heat. In a heatproof bowl, combine the egg yolks, sugar, and cornstarch and whisk until smooth. Slowly whisk in the hot milk until thoroughly blended. Return the egg-yolk mixture to the saucepan and place over medium heat. Cook, whisking constantly, until the mixture comes to a boil and thickens, about 3 minutes. Continue cooking, stirring constantly, for 1 minute longer to cook. Pour the custard through a sieve into a bowl. Stir in the butter, lemon zest and juice, and vanilla. Press a piece of plastic wrap onto the surface of the custard to prevent a skin from forming and poke a few holes in the plastic with the tip of a knife to allow steam to escape. Refrigerate until well chilled, for at least 2 hours or up to overnight.

BANANA CUSTARD

1 cup whole milk

3 large egg yolks

⅓ cup granulated sugar

4 teaspoons cornstarch

2 tablespoons unsalted butter, at room temperature

2 ripe bananas, mashed

1 teaspoon vanilla extract

MAKES ABOUT 1½ CUPS

In a saucepan over medium heat, warm the milk until small bubbles appear along the edges of the pan. Remove from the heat. In a heatproof bowl, combine the egg yolks, sugar, and cornstarch and whisk until smooth. Slowly whisk in the hot milk until blended. Return the egg-yolk mixture to the saucepan and place over medium heat. Cook, whisking constantly, until the mixture comes to a boil and thickens, about 3 minutes. Continue cooking, stirring constantly, for 1 minute longer to cook completely. Pour the custard through a fine-mesh sieve into a clean bowl. Stir in the butter, bananas, and vanilla. Press a piece of plastic wrap directly onto the surface of the custard to prevent a skin from forming and poke a few holes in the plastic with the tip of a knife to allow steam to escape. Refrigerate until well chilled, for at least 2 hours or up to overnight.

CHOCOLATE GANACHE

1 cup heavy cream

1 tablespoon unsalted butter

9 oz bittersweet chocolate, finely chopped

1 teaspoon vanilla extract

MAKES ABOUT 2½ CUPS

In a saucepan over low heat, combine the cream and butter and heat, stirring, until the butter is melted, tiny bubbles form, and the mixture is hot but not boiling (175°F on an instant-read thermometer). Remove from the heat, add the chocolate, and let stand for about 30 seconds to allow the chocolate to soften. Whisk until the chocolate is melted and the ganache is smooth. Stir in the vanilla. Pour the ganache into a metal bowl and use right away.

MEYER LEMON GLAZE

6 tablespoons unsalted butter, melted

2½ cups confectioners' sugar

2 tablespoons fresh Meyer lemon juice

3 tablespoons hot water, plus more as needed

½ teaspoon grated Meyer lemon zest

MAKES ABOUT 3 CUPS

In a bowl, whisk together the melted butter, confectioners' sugar, lemon juice, and 3 tablespoons hot water until smooth. Whisk in 1–2 teaspoons more hot water if needed to give the glaze a thin consistency. Stir in the lemon zest. Use right away.

ORANGE-FLOWER GLAZE

6 tablespoons unsalted butter, melted

2½ cups confectioners' sugar

1 teaspoon vanilla extract

¾ teaspoon orange-flower water

5 tablespoons hot water, plus more as needed

MAKES ABOUT 3 CUPS

In a bowl, whisk together the melted butter, confectioners' sugar, vanilla, orange-flower water, and 5 tablespoons hot water until smooth. Whisk in 1–2 teaspoons more hot water if needed to give the glaze a thin, light consistency. Use right away.

CINNAMON-ORANGE GLAZE

2 cups confectioners' sugar

1 teaspoon ground cinnamon

1 teaspoon light corn syrup

1 teaspoon grated orange zest

3 tablespoons hot water, plus more as needed

MAKES ABOUT 2½ CUPS

In a bowl, stir together the confectioners' sugar, cinnamon, corn syrup, orange zest, and 3 tablespoons hot water until well blended. Stir in 1–2 teaspoons more hot water if needed to give the glaze a thin, light consistency. Use right away.

CINNAMON-APPLE GLAZE

1 cup confectioners' sugar

½ teaspoon ground cinnamon

2 tablespoons apple cider or apple juice, plus more as needed

MAKES ABOUT 1¼ CUPS

In a bowl, stir together the confectioners' sugar, cinnamon, and 2 tablespoons apple cider until well blended. Stir in 1–2 teaspoons more cider if needed to make a smooth glaze that is easy to spread but thick enough to cling to the donuts. Use right away.

CINNAMON GLAZE

6 tablespoons unsalted butter, melted

2½ cups confectioners' sugar

1 teaspoon ground cinnamon

1 teaspoon vanilla extract

5 tablespoons hot water, plus more as needed

MAKES ABOUT 3 CUPS

In a bowl, whisk together the melted butter, confectioners' sugar, cinnamon, vanilla, and 5 tablespoons hot water until smooth. Whisk in 1–2 teaspoons more hot water if needed to give the glaze a thin, light consistency. Use right away.

COCONUT GLAZE

6 tablespoons unsalted butter, melted

2½ cups confectioners' sugar

1 teaspoon vanilla extract

½ teaspoon coconut extract

5 tablespoons hot water, plus more as needed

MAKES ABOUT 3 CUPS

In a bowl, whisk together the melted butter, confectioners' sugar, vanilla and coconut extracts, and 5 tablespoons hot water until smooth. Whisk in 1–2 teaspoons more hot water if needed to give the glaze a thin, light consistency. Use right away.

VANILLA GLAZE

6 tablespoons unsalted butter, melted

2½ cups confectioners' sugar

1 teaspoon vanilla extract

5 tablespoons hot water, plus more as needed

MAKES ABOUT 3 CUPS

In a bowl, whisk together the melted butter, confectioners' sugar, vanilla, and 5 tablespoons hot water until smooth. Whisk in 1–2 teaspoons more hot water if needed to give the glaze a thin, light consistency. Use right away.

THICK VANILLA GLAZE

2 cups confectioners' sugar

1 teaspoon light corn syrup

1 teaspoon vanilla extract

3 tablespoons hot water, plus more as needed

MAKES ABOUT 2 CUPS

In a bowl, stir together the confectioners' sugar, corn syrup, vanilla, and 3 tablespoons hot water. Stir in 1–2 teaspoons more hot water if needed to make a smooth glaze that is easy to spread but thick enough to cling to the donuts. Use right away.

MAPLE GLAZE

1 cup confectioners' sugar

¼ cup pure maple syrup

3 tablespoons heavy cream

MAKES ABOUT 2 CUPS

In a bowl, stir together the confectioners' sugar and maple syrup until well blended. Add the cream and whisk until smooth. Add a few more drops of cream or water if needed to make a smooth glaze that is easy to spread but thick enough to cling to the bars. Use right away.

CARAMEL GLAZE

¾ cup heavy cream

1 cup plus 2 tablespoons firmly packed light brown sugar

3 tablespoons light corn syrup

½ teaspoon salt

1 teaspoon vanilla extract

MAKES ABOUT 2 CUPS

In a heavy saucepan over medium heat, combine the cream, brown sugar, and corn syrup and heat, stirring often, until the brown sugar is dissolved and the mixture is smooth. Raise the heat to medium-high, bring to a boil, and cook, stirring constantly, for 2 minutes. Remove from the heat and stir in the salt and vanilla. Set aside and let stand at room temperature; the glaze will thicken as it cools. (The glaze will keep, covered in the refrigerator, for up to 2 days.) If the glaze is cold, reheat gently over low heat just until soft enough to spread.

STICKY TOFFEE GLAZE

1 cup heavy cream

¾ cup firmly packed dark brown sugar

1 teaspoon molasses

MAKES ABOUT 1¼ CUPS

In a saucepan over medium heat, combine the cream, brown sugar, and molasses and bring to a gentle boil, stirring to dissolve the brown sugar. Cook, uncovered, stirring often, until the mixture is reduced to about 1¼ cups, about 30 minutes. Adjust the heat as needed to maintain a gentle boil (just several large bubbles breaking the surface). Remove from the heat and set the sauce aside at room temperature to cool, about 1 hour. Use right away

CHOCOLATE GLAZE

⅓ cup heavy cream

4 tablespoons unsalted butter, cut into ½-inch cubes

3 tablespoons light corn syrup

4 oz semisweet chocolate, finely chopped

1 teaspoon vanilla extract

MAKES ABOUT 1 CUP

In a saucepan over medium heat, combine the heavy cream, butter, and corn syrup and cook, stirring, until the butter melts and the mixture is hot but not boiling. Remove the pan from the heat and add the chocolate. Let stand for about 30 seconds, then stir until the chocolate is completely melted and the glaze is smooth. Stir in the vanilla. Let the glaze cool until thickened, about 20 minutes. Use right away.

ESPRESSO GLAZE

2 cups confectioners' sugar

2 teaspoons instant espresso powder
dissolved in 2 teaspoons water

1 teaspoon light corn syrup

¼ teaspoon vanilla extract

3 tablespoons hot water, plus more as needed

MAKES ABOUT 2½ CUPS

In a bowl, stir together the confectioners' sugar,
espresso, corn syrup, vanilla, and 3 tablespoons
hot water until well blended. Stir in 1–2 teaspoons
more hot water if needed to make a smooth glaze
that is easy to spread but thick enough to cling to
the donuts. Use right away.

ALMOND CRUNCH

1 large egg white

1¼ cups sliced almonds

2 tablespoons granulated sugar

MAKES ABOUT 1½ CUPS

Preheat the oven to 325°F. Line a rimmed baking
sheet with parchment paper. In a bowl, whisk the
egg white until foamy, about 30 seconds. Add
the almonds and stir to coat them evenly with
the egg white. Sprinkle the sugar evenly over the
nuts and stir to mix well. Spread the nuts into a
single layer on the prepared baking sheet. Bake,
stirring once, until the nuts look golden and dry,
about 15 minutes. Remove from the oven and stir
the nuts to loosen them from the paper. Let cool
on the baking sheet; the nuts will become crisp as
they cool. Use right away.

SUGAR-AND-SPICE TOPPING

½ cup sugar

1½ teaspoons freshly ground pepper

1 teaspoon grated lemon zest

1 teaspoon kosher or sea salt

MAKES ABOUT ¾ CUP

In a wide, shallow bowl, combine the sugar,
pepper, lemon zest, and salt and stir to mix until
combined. Use right away.

STREUSEL TOPPING

¾ cup all-purpose flour

⅓ cup granulated sugar

⅓ cup firmly packed light brown sugar

½ teaspoon ground cinnamon

¼ teaspoon salt

4 tablespoons unsalted butter, melted

MAKES ABOUT 1½ CUPS

In a large bowl, stir together the flour, granulated
sugar, brown sugar, cinnamon, and salt. Add the
melted butter and stir just until crumbs form and
the mixture is evenly moistened. Use right away.

INDEX

weldon**owen**

1045 Sansome Street, San Francisco, CA 94111

weldonowen.com

LITTLE TREATS: DONUTS

Copyright © 2018 Weldon Owen International
All rights reserved, including the right of
reproduction in whole or in part in any form.

Printed in China
First printed in 2018
10 9 8 7 6 5 4 3 2 1

Library of Congress
Cataloging-in-Publication data is available.

ISBN: 978-1-68188-429-5

WELDON OWEN INTERNATIONAL

President & Publisher Roger Shaw
SVP, Sales & Marketing Amy Kaneko

Associate Publisher Amy Marr
Senior Editor Lisa Atwood

Creative Director Kelly Booth
Art Director Marisa Kwek
Senior Designer Meghan Hildebrand

Production Director Michelle Duggan
Imaging Manager Don Hill

ACKNOWLEDGMENTS

Weldon Owen wishes to thank the following people for their
generous support in producing this book: Lou Bustamante and Elizabeth Parson.

Elinor Klivans is an award-winning pastry chef trained in France and the United States. She is the author of several cookbooks, including *Big Fat Cookies* and *Bake and Freeze Desserts*, a Julia Child Cookbook Award nominee, and a coauthor of Williams Sonoma *Essentials of Baking*. Klivans is also a frequent guest on radio and television and has written for numerous national magazines.

Nancy Pappas is a graphic designer, illustrator, and passionate world traveler. She spends most of her time illustrating, researching, and fearlessly taste-testing food around the world. She has been featured in *Cherry Bombe* magazine and contributes to *Edible Queens*, *Counter Service*, and several other small publications. Her instagram, @nkpcreate, is an illustrated food journal documenting her international inspirations. Nancy is a Kansas City, Missouri transplant currently living in Brooklyn, New York.